SEXISM
IN HIGHER
EDUCATION

SEXISM
IN HIGHER
EDUCATION

Betty Richardson

A CONTINUUM BOOK
The Seabury Press · New York

The Seabury Press
815 Second Avenue
New York, N.Y. 10017

Copyright © 1974 by Betty Richardson
Designed by Paula Wiener
Printed in the United States of America

LIBRARY OF CONGRESS CATALOGING IN PUBLICATION DATA

Richardson, Betty, 1935–
   Sexism in higher education.

   (A Continuum book)
   An expansion of the author's paper, The happy hooker in the classroom, presented at the 1972 St. Louis convention of the Midwest Modern Language Association, and published in the spring issue, 1973, of the Association's Bulletin.
   1. Women college teachers.   2. Sex discrimination in education.
I.   Title.
LB2332.3.R52   1975   378.1'2   74–11103
ISBN 0–8164–9233–6

To my husband, John Adkins Richardson, professor of fine arts at Southern Illinois University, Edwardsville, and to my son, Victor Lewis Crain, because, if more academic men shared their concern with human knowledge and human dignity, there would be no real need for a book such as this.

Contents

SEXISM
IN HIGHER
EDUCATION

Preface

Like Becky Sharp in Thackeray's *Vanity Fair*, I early learned that my moral character would be vastly improved by financial solvency. Since then, seeking creature comforts, I have lived many lives and played many roles, most of them in some way connected with higher education. This book is the product of my experiences as student, graduate student, and student wife; as faculty member and faculty wife; as newspaper reporter and society editor in a university community; as a feminist, involved with both local and national organizations; as a person involved in the examination of grievances, especially in my work with the American Association of University Professors at both local and national levels; and as a woman, listening to other women late into the night, over Scotch and cigarettes, at a never-ending series of professional meetings and conventions. While I have relied, perhaps too heavily, upon previously published studies of education and of chauvinism in education, I have tried here to synthesize data, insights gleaned from literature and biography, and personal recollections of victimized women with my own experience, acquired painfully over the years, in order to produce an overview of academic chauvinism, and how and why it occurs.

I am not a radical feminist. So I believe, and so I am assured at regular intervals by my radical friends. Rather the point of view expressed here is that of a somewhat Victorian or *fin-de-siècle* humanist. I believe in the possibilities of higher education. Defined as the unbiased and dispassionate search for truth and knowledge, education, like Christianity, is simply a system that has too seldom been attempted. I believe in human freedom and in academic freedom, and I abhor party lines, including that of doctrinaire radical feminism. I also believe that the future of higher education and the future of American women are more completely interrelated than either educators or feminists are willing to admit. These attitudes underlie this book.

The present work originated as a paper entitled "The Happy Hooker in the Classroom: Female Rights and Professional Responsibilities," presented at the 1972 St. Louis convention of the Midwest Modern Language Association and subsequently published in the Spring 1973 issue of the *Bulletin of the Midwest Modern Language Association*. Then as now its purpose was to show, through the use of admittedly inadequate stereotypes, the ways in which women create their own problems in pursuing a career in education. In expanding the paper, however, I have been able to bring forward two other vital points: first, how educators are largely responsible for a climate in which bright women are predestined to failure, although educators are among the first to laugh at such failures; and, second, how the troubles of deeply disturbed professional women are related to childhood conditioning and to the tattered and outworn, but doggedly retained, preconceptions as to Everywoman's proper behavior.

Finally, I must acknowledge the debt I owe to a number of people. Justus George Lawler of Seabury Press offered both encouragement and practical help in transforming the paper into a full-length work. Dr. Carol Keene, chairman of the Department of Philosophical Studies at Southern Illinois University, Edwardsville, and Dr. Barbara Lawrence of their English Department were of invaluable assistance in helping me work out some of my ideas. I owe thanks, too, to many grievants, whose professional reputation might be jeopardized by any naming of names here. Professors Bernice Slote and Louis Crompton of the English Department at the University of Nebraska, my former teachers, have shown me by their example how idealism is best put into action. Nor could this book have been written without the atmosphere of academic freedom fostered at Southern Illinois University, Edwardsville, by President John S. Rendleman and Provost Andrew J. Kochman. My causes have frequently been unpopular; my argumentation, heated. Nonetheless, my participation in university affairs has been extensive, and I have so far thrived, completely free from any sense of constraint. In comparing notes with women from other institutions, I have come to realize how rarely colleagues of my sex enjoy such freedom and participation.

Introduction

"Home is the girl's prison and the woman's workhouse," wrote George Bernard Shaw in 1903.[1] It still is. Of all the movements toward egalitarianism that followed the French Revolution, feminism has progressed most slowly. It is true that feminists have not generally had to face lynch mobs or nightriders who burned crosses on their front lawns. Nevertheless, they have faced a sustained hostility and resentment which in intensity invite comparison with the pathological obstructionism that crippled the working man in the nineteenth century and the black man in the twentieth. Almost two hundred years after Mary Wollstonecraft's famous lament as to the ill-breeding and incompetent education of women—leading, inevitably, to their domestic dependency, intellectual inferiority, frivolity, and occasional mindlessness—the vast majority of women still exist amidst conditions that Wollstonecraft would recognize and that form the gist of her complaint in *A Vindication of the Rights of Woman* (1792).

Nowhere is resistance to feminine freedom more obvious than in academic life. It is a truism of current feminist writings that higher education long has offered the most agreeable haven for women in full flight from the debacles of domesticity. Yet in a 1971 survey of 418 college and university language departments, the Modern Language Association Commission on the Status of Women in the Profession showed that, in university life and even in those disciplines that emphasize verbal skills in which women demonstrably excel, women—the few who are hired—tend to remain at the bottom of the academic hierarchy. Women make up 49 per cent of instructors and lecturers in modern language departments, but only 7 per cent of full professors are female. The study, reports the Commission, engendered a "guarded optimism." [2] One wonders why.

Optimism seems even less justified in light of the general academic employment picture. A more recent study of college and university employment shows that female appointments rose a mere nine-tenths of one percentage point (from 19.1 to 20 per cent) between 1968 and 1972, despite new Affirmative Action guidelines and increased pressure, often through the courts, for their implementation. [3] Salaries, too, continue to reflect sexual bias. According to a 1968 survey, 19 per cent of men employed in colleges and universities earn $17,000 or more, as compared with 4 per cent of the women; [4] and there is little reason to believe that the situation has changed much during the past six years. The picture is further complicated by a decline, in recent years, in the number of professionally qualified women in certain fields. For example, there is evidence of a decrease in the number of doctorates granted women in some of the physical and biological sciences, and the number of female mathematicians dropped sharply between 1950 and 1960.[5] It is significant, too, that Caroline Bird reports a 1 per cent decline between 1930 and 1967 in the number of women listed in *Who's Who in America*.[6]

The implication is that women continue to enter a limited range of fields—English, foreign languages, developmental and school psychology—where they will end by competing against each other for a limited number of positions. Such fields become occupational ghettoes for women, just as, in the world outside, women tend to cluster as underpaid librarians, saleswomen, waitresses, secretaries, barmaids, and social workers. So far little has been done to break down the ghetto walls. When a field such as nursing gains in money and status, it is seemingly because men are beginning to enter that discipline. The apparent gains seldom have anything to do with the upgrading of women professionals—as women.

Further, the situation threatens to grow much worse. During the past two years, there is increasing evidence that talented and ambitious women, especially feminists, are being squeezed out of the profession altogether, their dismissals weakly justified under frequently unproven conditions of "fiscal exigency." (Those who remain will be the placid and the timorous, content forever to be underpaid and overworked.) The number of these terminations may be expected to rise so long as economic retrenchment continues to provide an excuse. Moreover, even in a time of plenty, professional women are unwelcome. They are no better received when they appear to be competing with

husbands and fathers for a dwindling pool of jobs in an
intensely competitive market. Already husbands and
fathers among faculty members seem to be conniving
with administrators in many of the more flagrantly
discriminatory terminations, for the sake of guaranteeing
their own jobs and improving their own salaries. This
bodes ill, too, for that slightly greater number of women
who have entered graduate school in the early 1970's, under the impetus of the new feminism. Some have already
found that, although Affirmative Action investigators can
pressure chairmen into offering "courtesy" interviews to
more women than previously, the chairmen and their colleagues will still find excuses to hire only men.

Almost as shocking is the fact that academic feminists
have been no great source of consolation and advice. Much
feminist writing remains utterly irrelevant to practical life.
Often feminists merely aggravate an already ugly situation.
Also it does not help matters that many have rejected disciplined logic and prose as "masculine" and "establishment," producing, instead, emotive and often incompre-
hensible treatises that even a thoughtful feminist is hard-
pressed to defend when males offer them up as further
evidence of feminine intellectual inferiority. Among the
better-trained rebels, many have unwittingly retained all
the bad habits of the disciplines in which they were reared,
so that their writings are impenetrably verbose or hopelessly opaque in their dependence upon the currently
fashionable jargon of some narrow discipline.

The best of current writings are purely scholarly or the-
oretical, or they are primarily informational sourcebooks.
Such works as Katharine M. Rogers's *The Troublesome
Helpmate* provide excellent scholarly backgrounds for

studies of the roles of women in Western culture, while Elizabeth Janeway, in *Man's World, Woman's Place,* brilliantly offers a theoretical foundation for future studies of women within the social sciences, literature, and the arts. Two recent collections of essays, *And Jill Came Tumbling After,* edited by Judith Stacey, Susan Bereaud, and Joan Daniels, and *Academic Women on the Move,* edited by Alice Rossi and Ann Calderwood, are superb sourcebooks, guaranteed to dispel any lingering doubts concerning woman's subservient position in American education.[7] But of necessity these works remain largely aloof from the simple problems of everyday life.

More frustrating are those feminists who are permanently sidetracked. Some, aiming at biological or anthropological profundity, seem fixated upon role-models provided by the female praying mantis or the baboon, when they are not extolling the sexual habits of South Sea islanders or postulating a prehistoric matriarchy, possibly populated by beings from other planets. Though sometimes intellectually fascinating, these studies, as should be self-evident, are of limited practical application.

Still they at least avoid the havoc that has been wrought by the written products of radical centers in New York, Washington, D.C., Los Angeles, and Chicago. Mostly these latter are noteworthy for their intolerance of and contempt for less enlightened sisters. By terrorizing the run-of-the-mill woman, they have served to postpone unduly a grass-roots feminist movement, even among academic women. Most academic women are reformists, not revolutionaries. Most cannot adapt to a feminism that demands, as part of any basic commitment, the overthrow of the U.S. government or the Christian religion. Dedicated to intellectual activities, they are appalled by the anti-intellectual spirit of many of these writings and find the intellectual life of Russia or Communist China, held forth by some radicals as idealized models for the future, to be on the whole a rather depressing spectacle. Still others witness with some dismay the tendency of radicals to confuse economic and sexual matters, often vehemently insisting that the road to freedom lies in sexual promiscuity, the dissolution of all marriages, or the rejection of all males. To women concerned with problems of bread-and-butter survival, discussions of these matters—or of body hair, porno films for women, and lesbianism—suggest that feminists are not really interested in women. Rather these are women of leisure and substance, interested solely in an equally privileged audience, frequently with the somewhat childish object of shocking their parents and their parents' generation.

Ultimately, however, the wavering economics of the 1970's will have a healthy effect upon academic feminism. As economic life becomes more perilous, a new kind of woman is being forced into the feminist fold. Labor-union women and black women can no longer be ignored, especially as educational groups become entangled in collective bargaining and as black women are given prestigious, if too often token, appointments in academic administrations. These new women, if they can no longer afford to exist in a man's world, neither are they prepared to tolerate much nonsense from their sisters; and their presence is forcing a greater acknowledgment of individual life styles. Already younger women are questioning some earlier presuppositions. That personal freedom is related to indiscriminate sexual activity, whether heterosexual or homosexual, has been challenged by Nancy Press Hawley and her co-authors in *Our Bodies, Ourselves,* in which these women conclude that pressures to enjoy sex "with impunity, without anxiety, under any conditions and with anyone" have proven "no less destructive or degrading than the Victorian puritanism we all so proudly rejected." [8] Simultaneously, Carolyn Heilbrun's *Toward a Recognition of Androgyny* marks a breakthrough both in the use of humanistic materials in feminist analysis and in the admission of individualized needs and differences. [9]

The movement should force reassessment of basic issues, among which is the determination of what is meant by freedom. Economic independence, of course, is fundamental. As Virginia Woolf long ago noted, no woman can be free until she can afford a room of her own, [10] and she will feel demeaned so long as she must coyly entice or accept money from husband, brother, father, employer, or even social worker at the welfare office, as if it is a gift and not rightfully earned. Here increased governmental pressures are essential. But the rest is dependent upon the individual woman's skills and knowledge and upon her control of her body, emotions, and intellect. While the federal government can force a given institution to hire and to retain a certain number of women, it is a rather different matter to ensure the continued employment of any particular individual. Today an intelligent and competent instructor can expect that somewhere she will be denied tenure, but there also exists a phenomenon that might be called the Untenured Personality, which bears a strange resemblance to the perennially unemployed waitress or salesclerk or dishwasher. This woman's basic problem, as she wanders from job to job, is that she is ignorant of essential skills, lacks emotional maturity, and is sometimes even unaware of those minimal decencies that allow human beings to survive in an overcrowded society without murdering each other any more often than they do. (The male version of the Untenured Personality will sabotage any job opportunity within 24 hours of his arrival by pinching a female administrator on the thigh, in what he considers an amiable and even affectionate manner, or by patting a black nationalist on his Afro, murmuring: "I'm sure going to enjoy working with you, boy.") In its most extreme form, the Untenured Personality would raise the hackles of even the most pacifist and uncompetitive of South Sea islanders. Freedom is contingent, unfortunately, not only upon general cultural attitudes but upon the individual's autonomy, sensitivity, and sense of responsibility.

And this leads to the second basic issue, the need to accept responsibility for one's actions. Once upon a time, little girls learned that, if they did not brush their teeth or eat their turnips, "They" would be displeased. Children were never allowed to ask who "They" were or why "Their" opinions mattered. The more recent and slightly more sophisticated version of the game is to posit "Men" or "Society" as the controlling agent of all that happens, as if the unfortunate socialization of women were an absolutely irreversible process. This is a particularly odd stance for academic women since, if behavior and knowledge are irrevocably fixed in childhood, there is no point in funding universities in the first place. What has *not* been stressed of late is that self-awareness, the absence of which Karl Menninger has recently chosen to term sin:[11] the simple admission that actions have consequences. When the consequences are demonstrably undesirable, there remains the option of changing the action. There is no question that cultural chauvinism is a reality. Nonetheless those feminist consciousness-raising groups that are content with finding societal or masculine scapegoats are merely evading some equally real problems, not solving them—which is probably why such groups tend to dissolve rather quickly.

Only by acknowledging the importance of personal responsibility can one come to terms with the third issue, the definition of personal integrity. Turning social conventions upside down will not free one from those conventions, nor will it result in a well-defined, autonomous personality. Nor does integrity evolve from blind adherence to a party line, whether it be that of radical feminism or gray-haired senior professors. The required sense of strength and internal consistency can arise only from self-knowledge, sometimes painfully acquired, and from self-acceptance, sometimes possible only at the cost of unlearning certain patterns of behavior established in childhood. For it is true that ghastly things happen to girls, especially girls who are bright. Inadvertently, they accept certain archetypal roles, most of which are ultimately self-destructive.

Five such stereotyped roles appear with monotonous regularity among academic women. Of course, all such descriptions are oversimplifications, most personalities being much more rich and varied than the following descriptions suggest. Stereotypes are simply not real people. Yet, amidst the chaos of human behavior, some patterns do recur. Among them are:

1. *Circe.* Circe is the eternal enchantress. In Homer's *Odyssey* she is that *femme fatale* who lures men only to

change them to swine. Just below the surface of Circe's usually glamorous exterior, there is a deep sexual hostility of which she frequently is unconscious. Yet it is likely to influence her every professional action.

2. *Medea.* In classical myth and drama Medea leaves behind, in the wake of her peregrinations, a striking configuration of boiled bodies, mangled limbs, and butchered infants. Some sociologists have christened her modern counterpart the Queen Bee, but that hardly does justice to her terrible anger.

3. *Medusa.* According to tradition, Medusa's every glance changes men to stone. Her round face is ugly, her hair a tangle of snakes, and her teeth those of a boar. Under the circumstances she would seem more sinned against than sinning. Unfortunately, no one told *her* that.

4. *Penelope.* Penelope, waiting for Odysseus to return from his long voyage, comes down through history as a crashing bore. She epitomizes the womanly virtues, unraveling each day's weaving so that her woman's work is never done. She is a bit of a nuisance in a heroic poem, as in a modern university.

5. *Hebe.* Slim, perennially adolescent Hebe is cupbearer to the gods. Her spiritual descendants nurture drug freaks, renegade radicals, and middle-aged professors whose wives fail to understand them.

So basic are these archetypal role-models that they go unquestioned, although they have long outworn their social usefulness. Yet feminism is dependent not only upon long overdue reforms of academic institutions, but on freeing individuals from these emotional Procrustes' beds to which they desperately and misguidedly seem to cling.

The nature of this conditioning, the interaction of the conditioned adult with an intensely chauvinistic educational system, and the resultant explosions—these form the subject of this book.

Part One

The Training
of the Combatants

1

Two Presuppositions
Concerning Conditioning

"My mother was right," asserts the narrator of Alix Kates Shulman's *Memoirs of an Ex-Prom Queen*. "There was only one way for a girl to control her future: choose her man." [1] "You aren't a nobody if a guy looks at you," says Simone Berteaut in her biography of her sister, *Piaf*, "you're alive." [2] Says Helen Gurley Brown: ". . . while you're waiting to marry, or if you never marry, a job can be your love, your happy pill, your means of finding out who you are." [3] Underlying these statements is a shared belief, namely, that women have no identity apart from that bestowed by male sanction. Little boys are asked what they "want" to be when they grow up, but even adult women, returning late in life to a career or to the classroom, can rarely verbalize their futures in terms of their "wants," having since childhood learned a list of "oughts" and "shoulds," the goal of which is male approval.

It is assumed that, when the girl has done as she "ought,"

this approval will naturally follow, and the girl will know what she is—she is a "good girl." She knows she has been approved when she is elected cheerleader or voted queen of the prom or when she finds what will be viewed in her cultural group as a high-status husband. Despite much publicized alternative life styles, Marcia Seligson, in her recent, cynical exploration of American matrimonial customs, finds that a substantial number of girls retain these highly conventional attitudes; she herself recalls that she spent much of her childhood drawing pictures of bridal gowns by the hour.[4] Unfortunately, even the girl who achieves conventional rewards is now confronted with new long-range problems. In the past half-century, a woman's life expectancy has increased by some 30 to 35 years, so that she must now face several additional decades in which no one will think to reward her for anything. Swaying over her martini at the country club or muttering over her beer in a sawdust bar—or storming at her husband over faculty-club sherry—she seems to serve no useful purpose except to keep countless bartenders, psychiatrists, lawyers, and marriage counsellors off the public dole. Even more tragic, however, is the woman who has never felt admired or indispensable or enjoyed much social approval; and traditionally she has sought refuge in the cloistered halls of academe. As Alice Rossi has observed, this woman has a "special need" for recognition and approbation, as compensation for emotional deprivations that have continued since childhood.[5]

For it is as abnormal today for a girl's intelligence to be praised as it was in the 1880's, and it is equally abnormal for a woman to pursue a career. It is normal for women to work, but only under conditions of continuing squalor.

(The median salary for the more than 40 per cent of American women in the work force was, in 1971, about $4000, compared to more than $8000 for males. Hugh Maccool, legislative advocate for California Clerical and Allied Services Employees, reports that as many as 11.5 per cent of that state's 30,000 clerical workers may qualify for welfare and that, indeed, many single and separated women must supplement their salaries with welfare stipends in order to survive.[6]) Apart from the numbers of women involved, their situation has changed little in the last century. A talented and gifted woman will be made to feel abnormal in her girlhood; and she will be made to regard herself as no less of an untouchable or oddity as a professor.

Her sense of abnormality is contingent upon cultural acceptance of two myths. The first of these is the concept of a happy marriage and nuclear family, evolved from mankind's recurrent desire to locate some golden age in the not too distant past—and to return to that age directly. A closely related concept is that of the female as happy sufferer. If it is true that modern man retains a primitive fear of "magic" or "sacred" female fecundity, then this myth may well be related to the age-old stories of scapegoat gods, divine figures who cheerfully allowed themselves to be sacrificed that the earth might be renewed. More prosaically, it may have evolved as a simple rationalization, allowing men to escape an overwhelming burden of guilt brought about by the sight of woman's pain in childbirth.[7] Or it may merely be a power play.

Whatever the source, there is no scarcity of intellectually committed academicians to reassert regularly the prevalence of happy marriage—and if marriages were not always happy, that did not matter because woman is naturally masochistic anyhow. And every year some new voice—most recently that of George Gilder[8]—preaches the need for a quick return to this largely mythological golden age. Thus there is no way of attacking conventional feminine conditioning without first arguing against these suppositions upon which the conditioning rests. And the easiest way to attack these suppositions is to ask that a closer look be taken at family life as it actually existed during the allegedly golden ages of Victorian and Edwardian domestic bliss.

One finds, first of all, that domesticity was categorically rejected by those families who could afford whatever variety of bliss they chose. As Anita Leslie has recorded in *The Marborough House Set*, the adulterous marriage of convenience was an accepted institution by the turn of the century, an institution so well known as to be satirized by Elinor Glyn in one of her popular novels, *Visits of Elizabeth*, in 1900, the year of Queen Victoria's death. Nor does the concept of happy marriage quite explain the large number of famous and expensive Victorian courtesans— Cora Pearl, Hortense Schneider—who were publicly recognized by correspondents in such stolid newspapers as the London *Times*. On this side of the Atlantic, Fanny Kemble recorded, and later published, the horrors of marriage to a Southern plantation owner; while, according to the memoirs published by Elizabeth Lehr, marriage to a Northern leader of fashion was no better. Though viewing maternity through rose-tinted spectacles, even Jonathan Gathorne-Hardy cannot conceal his disgust in admitting that, throughout the golden age, women of wealth and culture cunningly contrived to avoid prolonged contact with their offspring.[9]

If the domestic ideal was not widely realized among the rich, neither was it realizable among the poor. From the age of agriculture through the age of cottage industry, working-men's wives had traditionally labored along side their men; and they continued to do so into the industrial age. Children, too, were put to work, often entering factories and mills at the age of five or six, and the 40-hour work week had not yet been devised. Even with every member employed, the family often earned merely a pittance that required them to subsist among conditions of abject squalor. According to an 1864 factory inspector's report, the "poorly-clad" wives evidenced a "glaring neglect or ignorance of home duties," and the children were "half-naked and half-starved." Among the poor, deaths from child neglect ran high; and after insurance programs were developed in the eighteenth century, it was not uncommon for impoverished parents to resort to an exceedingly primitive mode of population control. Insuring the lives of a superfluous infant or two, they then poisoned the children with the family opium supply. This was common, too, among the vast ranks of those who could find only occasional employment. Even more frequently, their children were simply dumped into the streets, to die or survive as best they could. In the London of the 1870's there may have been as many as 30,000 homeless street Arabs, few of them able to identify or to locate a living parent, while Jacob Riis reports a similar army of waifs in the slums of New York. Below this was another class. It is not surprising that female slaves were used as brood mares. Most women were. But the slave alone was forced to watch as her children were taken to be sold to other owners.[10]

All this is forgotten, of course, when the stable family is posited as a viable part of our cultural heritage. In point of fact, this notion was never much more than an ideal of the middle classes, and how seldom it was realized even there is suggested in the novels of Charles Dickens, Elizabeth Gaskell, and John Galsworthy, as well as in biographical and autobiographical accounts of Samuel Butler, John Stuart Mill, Virginia Woolf, Bernard Shaw, and Beverley Nichols. Significantly, Thomas Carlyle and John Ruskin, two of the most vehement Victorian defenders of this ideal, were haunted throughout their lives by rumors of their sexual impotence and of their fragile or unconsummated marriages. There is also Leon Edel's touching portrait of Alice James, gradually lapsing into hysteria and deep depression as a function of her boredom and helplessness in a middle-class American home. And Florence Nightingale, writing in 1853, testified: "It is surprising that there is so much love as there is. . . . Husbands and wives never seem to have anything to say to one another." [11]

If some women romanticized marriage, others—so Miss Nightingale insists—escaped into it as a means of evading their parents. For many others, prostitution and marriage were the only remunerative alternatives, and indeed that still is true. In the 1880's, Bernard Shaw observed in *Mrs. Warren's Profession* that work available to women is so unrewarding as to lead girls to "lung disease, premature death, and domestic desertion or brutality." This being the case, girls might as well choose the primrose path since "vice at worst and virtue at best, lead to the same end in poverty and overwork." [12] Many made that choice. In 1857 a medical journal reported that one of every 16 women in London was a prostitute, at least part-time; in 1868, some 6515 known prostitutes were reported, but estimates were to range as high as 83,000.[13] Almost a century later, "J," an informant for Kate Millett's *Prostitute Papers,* reiterated Shaw's argument. Why, she asked, should a girl settle for $5000 a year and an office job when as a prostitute she may earn as much as $50,000? [14]

Whatever her profession, the fact that she was female until recently guaranteed certain unpleasantnesses. Hazards of childbirth only gradually lessened. Having given birth to her fifth child in 1656, Alice Thornton records that "then a new trouble seized on me by the loss of blood, in the bleeding of the hemorrhoids every day for half a year together." [15] At the end of that century, Queen Anne survived more than 15 miscarriages and childbirths, seeing no child survive to inherit her throne. Mary Wollstonecraft was one of those multitudes who died in childbirth. Marie Antoinette was forced from her sickbed to her trial, despite the fact that she was suffering from excessive menstrual hemorrhages. (Caused by nerves? By tumors? Neither she nor her doctors could have known.) Even in 1853, when Queen Victoria requested newly discovered chloroform at her next confinement, she stirred many preachers of her kingdom to wrath. Some argued that a woman's sufferings in labor were responsible for her love of her children. Others pointed out that, in the pains of childbirth, women atoned for the sins of Eve in the Garden of Eden. Nevertheless, Victoria persisted. Her rejection of pain as woman's divinely appointed lot may have been her finest gift to the people of her kingdom.[16]

Repeated pregnancies were necessary, for infant mortality remained relatively high. A monthly mortality bill, printed in 1736 in a London journal, lists the deaths of 1054 children under two years of age, in contrast to only 103 deaths among persons aged 70 to 80.[17] If G. M. Young's statistics are to be taken seriously, life expectancy in the English industrial towns of Manchester and Liverpool was 20 and 22 years respectively among traders and farmers at the beginning of the nineteenth century, and 17 and 15 years among laborers.[18] In 1850, according to Laver, death claimed 10 per cent of infants born to the upper classes, 15 per cent among the middle classes, and 30 per cent among the poor.[19] Even toward the end of the century, when Florence Nightingale investigated conditions in maternity hospitals, she found that, in one Paris hospital, the maternal death rate was 193.7 per thousand deliveries.[20]

The list continues. Neither sanitary napkins nor tampons had yet been invented. Breast and cervical cancers frequently went undiagnosed, and there was little to be done in any case. Venereal disease, too, was difficult to detect among women, as it is today. Frequently, it was brought home to women who had never even heard about it by men who were in no position to explain. Even diabetes, often aggravated by pregnancy, was untreatable until the discovery of insulin and its purification for use on human patients in 1922. Until the common use of antibiotics after the Second World War, there was equally little to be done about even common vaginal and bladder infections, except to let them run their natural and usually not very pleasant course. And the change from ghastly or at least unsanitary methods of birth control—early Egyptian women apparently used crocodile dung—to more predictable techniques, less likely to cause septic conditions, needs hardly be mentioned.

There is no particularly good reason to believe that women revelled in all this, any more than most of them delighted in the laws that denied them basic civil rights. The nineteenth century was a socially conscious age. Unable to cope with problems that could not be simply solved by the enactment of a Reform Bill or Emancipation Proclamation, or the waging of a Civil War, it collectively chose to ignore the problem, much as the twentieth century has chosen to ignore the problems of age and death, so far as they refuse to yield to simplistic technological solutions. It might have been argued, too, that man's life was often brief and brutish and that, until late in the nineteenth century, many men had not yet realized that they might claim legal and civil rights. The natural unpleasantnesses that remained were obviously ordained by a divine or moral or natural order. Woman was simply to endure them and teach her daughters to do likewise. Not only did she in fact do just that but she still does, even when it is no longer necessary. But this does not mean that she craved to be more wretched and miserable, except that in some cases she believed that her forebearance would prove her worthier of God's grace.

It is in the pornographic tradition, in which the human male plays God, that the figure of the happy sufferer is developed. In real life she probably exists in no greater abundance than does the male masochist. The female figure came into full bloom in the eighteenth century with the development of the novel. There rape or threatened rape and the ambiguous responses of the victim form the theme for Samuel Richardson's *Pamela* (1740–1741) and his *Clarissa* (1747–1748) and for John Cleland's porno-graphic *Fanny Hill* or *Memoirs of a Woman of Pleasure* (1748–1749), as well as other less important works. In terms of what is known of the psychological convulsions of the eighteenth century, it is possible to interpret this theme as representative of stress within the mind of the creator. The "female" of such works is the soft—or ro-mantic or Dionysian—element of the psyche, to be beaten into shape by the masculine—or classic or Apollonian or rational—elements of which Western culture increasingly approved.

Whatever its function, the theme of happy sufferer quickly became a literary convention. Underground—al-though, in less titillating forms, it is evident in even the chastest and most domestic of Victorian household tales—it is still quite evident in the writings of Freud and in such pornographic titles as *Sadopaideia, Being the Experiences of Cecil Prendergast, Undergraduate of the University of Oxford, Showing How He Was Led Through the Pleasant Paths of Masochism to the Supreme Joys of Sadism.*[21]

When the figure surfaced again in the twentieth cen-tury, it was to be cynically exploited for unconsciously political purposes. Especially in the 1950's and 1960's, it has been most obvious in magazines and advertisements produced by men for women. Particularly is it evident in literature designed for the least educated and most gulli-ble of women. Every second headline on a true confes-sions or romance magazine seems to begin: "He Made Me Do. . . ," "He Forced Me. . . ," "Cornered With A Raging. . . ," or "Made Pregnant by a Psychopathic Killer." The purpose is no less political when the theme is exploited by Norman Mailer or by the producers of *Last*

Tango in Paris or *Deep Throat.* So long as one woman is still convinced that she should be a masochist, it will still be possible to discriminate against women on the ground of their natural subservience.

And this is why the myths are still propagated by academic men, who ought to know better. Their lives are based on certain myths; and to avoid destroying them, males in various disciplines have taken devious routes. Historians, for example, will refuse to examine anything outside the narrow limits of political or military history, when they are not preoccupied with the correction of usually trivial dates. Sociologists refuse to admit that the world existed before 1950. Psychologists seem alternately to commune with Sigmund Freud and white rats, while teachers of literature insist that discussion of a poem's or novel's social context would contaminate perception of literature as an aesthetic object. While there is virtue in all these approaches, such exclusive concentration also suggests a deeper problem, one that only a dose of feminist studies will be able to combat.

2

Preying Together

American homes are "damagingly matriarchal," writes Jane Howard in a recent survey of female life styles in the 1970's. There is something in them that "scares men away."[1] This, of course, is no new observation. Among many others, novelist Elinor Glyn, coming from England to Hollywood as a film writer, bemusedly remarked in the 1920's that "America is the woman's kingdom."[2] And, more recently, British anthropologist Eric John Dingwall observed the American home with something resembling horror. In his book on *The American Woman*, he cites a 1942 Dorothy Dix column, in which two sisters (ages 28 and 23) and a brother (26), signing themselves "Three Miserable Children," asked what to do about a mother who forbade them to drive in their own car or to bring guests into the house that they had paid for and from whom "they suffered a tongue-lashing whenever they went out in the evening."[3]

Presumably, in these homes, the mother is expected to teach the bliss of domesticity and the feminine virtues of passivity, docility, and patience. Certainly, there is evidence that the mother begins to help infants define behavior according to sex, even in the first several weeks after birth. The boy is encouraged to establish greater independence, while the girl is bound closely to her mother's side and is urged to accept her mother's oppressive presence as an indication of maternal love.[4]

What happens more often than not, however, is the establishment of a conflict situation in these first few years. This is especially true where the home itself is a battleground. In infancy the girl learns to hate or to distrust the home and everything it represents, so that later efforts to condition her to accept femininity and domesticity are doomed to an ignominious failure. Often academic women are recruited from among such girls, but they are not the only ones. In her autobiographical work *An Unfinished Woman*, playwright Lillian Hellman recalls a ping-pong existence between two parents "who certainly loved me for myself, but who also liked to use me against each other."[5] In an anthology of writings on lesbianism, Ann Aldrich interviewed a young homosexual nurse who first learned to conceptualize sex as a kind of "wrestling match" in which the mother was a bedraggled and reluctant participant.[6] Jack Olsen, in *The Girls in the Office*, records the sad if common recollections of 26-year-old "Vanessa Van Durant." Seeking the affection she never found in childhood through a frustratingly indiscriminate series of sexual adventures, the woman recalled a home life punctuated by the brawls of parents who fought and argued and slashed "with words and sometimes with other instruments." [7] These women have either deliberately rebelled against the role-model projected by the mother; or they have been crippled in some way so that, family and social pressures notwithstanding, they are unable to imitate her.

For cultural conditioning can only be effective when the girl retains some lingering affection and admiration for the mother, as is not always the case. Sometimes a close relationship is made impossible from birth, for the mother is too evidently disappointed when the infant is a daughter and not a son. In Radclyffe Hall's 1928 lesbian classic, *The Well of Loneliness*, the author describes a typical relationship between a young girl, starved for affection, and the mother who had wanted a boy. Stephen, the daughter, observes that her mother's eyes "would look cold, though her voice might be gentle, and her hand when it fondled would be tentative, unwilling." Looking into her mother's "calm, lovely face," the daughter "would be filled with a sudden contrition, with a sudden deep sense of her own shortcomings . . ." [8] Beatrice Webb also "hungered, hopelessly" through childhood for her mother's affection. The mother was bitterly resentful that a son had died, while little superfluous Beatrice continued to live on. [9] And the enduring effect on Marilyn Monroe of a mentally disturbed mother and of "near-mad" foster homes has been sensitively analyzed by Diana Trilling in her essay on "The Death of Marilyn Monroe." [10]

The mothers are not altogether to be blamed. For the past century, many of those who have been confined to the home have been making their own misery known, although few have listened. During the great wave of social consciousness in the last half of the nineteenth century, ladies found themselves to be the lilies of the field. They toiled not. Neither did they spin. Worst of all, they were not at all sure that God any longer rewarded that kind of thing. Thus Florence Nightingale found herself at the edge of a nervous breakdown, caught between her need to serve God and the frivolous demands of an unsatisfying social life. Beatrice Webb would fly from parties to her room in order to lecture herself over the banality of her existence. Since then, socialist ethics have increasingly influenced society, even where they have not dominated. Called on to justify their existences, ladies found they could not, especially as labor-saving devices have increased and as large families have become less desirable. As early as 1929, in *Middletown*, Robert S. Lynd and Helen Merrell Lynd noted that, of 112 working-class wives, only 27 managed to spend seven or more hours a day at housework; of 40 business-class wives, 31 spent less than seven hours.[11] As we know today, much of this time is spent in busy work, expanding and creating chores to fill idle hours. What Betty Friedan observed in *The Feminine Mystique* was not the beginning of a climate of despair, but its culmination. Even while the working woman was taught to despair at depriving her children of her full attentions, the woman of leisure was made to feel equally guilty. She had been taught that marriages were happy and housewives to be envied. If her marriage were dull and her life boring, the fault must be her own. Enmeshed in her own guilt and misery, she often had little emotional strength to offer to her daughter, nor did the child always see much that seemed worth imitating.

The inadvertent hypocrisy that resulted may have been largely responsible for the explosive, volatile nature of much 1970's feminism. Mother "knew" that daughter should be a good, normal woman, but she also "knew" that she herself was no such thing. To help daughter along, then, she must not rely on her own experience; she must seek her values in the world outside, mostly in mass media. There she finds pop psychology—the product of generations of hack journalists who reiterate the old Victorian domestic values—and advertisements that promise beauty and happiness with the use of a new kind of soap flake.

Most frequently, she seeks values in the domestic sentimentality of woman's fiction. It is not necessary to belabor here the stultifying stereotyping of such magazines as *McCalls* and the *Ladies' Home Journal,* but it is worth noting that domesticity is sentimentalized in other less likely genres. In science fiction, as Joanna Russ has pointed out, present values are projected even into "future Galactic Empires," in which good women still remain weak and beautiful—and passive.[12] Detective fiction, too, remains relatively untouched. While such novels as P. D. James's *An Unsuitable Job for a Woman* present a slightly modified female heroine, few writers have disputed Howard Haycraft's dictum that women and boys are not satisfactory as detectives.[13] When a woman appears in that role at all, there usually lurks, in the background, a sustaining and virile male mentor who comes to the rescue when the woman finds herself out of her own depth. And the changes that have been wrought by such academic thriller writers as Amanda Cross have been more than counterbalanced by the masochistic feminine role-models in the more popular series by Ian Fleming and Mickey Spillane. Then, too, there are the modern Gothic romances and the light novels of such perennial favorites as Emilie Loring, with their inevitably helpless heroines and orange-blossom endings.

Of late woman has also fallen victim to one last fraudulent attempt to convince her that her "useful" work can be expanded to fill a life. Obviously, this is the motivation underlying recent articles on macramé, home candle-making, and health foods, which have replaced the earlier ghastlinesses of do-it-yourself hat-trimming and painting-by-numbers. Macramé, of course, can be an art form. It rarely is. Moreover, there is a distinct limit as to how much of the stuff can be given away, worn, or strung about the house. Candles are luxuries today, whether one makes them or buys them. And while a health-food addict can tyrannize her family with wheat germ, she cannot control her husband's or children's dietary habits once they leave the home—and, given enough wheat germ, they leave rapidly and frequently. So she must feed them supplementary vitamins anyhow. As is quickly being discovered, these activities offer immediate satisfactions and long-range frustrations, especially when, as too often happens, the woman is so deluded as to believe that proficiency at them will allow her to earn a living should she be widowed or divorced.

But she grabs at these activities and at the values represented as at a life raft, and she brings them home to daughter. Granted an extremely placid domestic situation or a bovine child, daughter accepts them. It is just as likely, however, that daughter is merely puzzled. Unable to comprehend her mother's own desperate groping for help, she perceives only the vast gulf between what mother preaches and what she practices. Mother urges domestic

virtues and activities upon her daughter, but she rarely
is satisfied with them herself. Mother preaches the bliss
of marriage, but she herself is bored or miserable. She
urges that her daughter be happy in her role as a young
woman, but she herself is emotionally turbulent in her own
discontent. To the child this appears as hypocrisy. If the
child is already unhappy in the home, this is one more excuse to reject the mother and her world.

Daughter's rejection, of course, is perceived by the
mother as one more evidence of her own failure—something else to feel guilty about. And this may evoke a variety of other emotions. On the one hand, she may feel a
deep and genuine concern that the girl must learn to live
a "normal" life. In a more punitive and vengeful woman,
the same spirit may manifest itself as a grim determination
to force the girl into acceptance of the mother and the
mother's role at all costs. Whatever the motivation, she
will probably search for more gimmicks to help condition
the child into conformity. Merchandisers are more than
willing to help her in finding them. From a Christmas cata-
log, for example, she may choose any of almost a dozen
models of doll baby carriages, as well as kitchens, beauty
parlors, boutiques, and furniture. One Barbie Doll can even
hold hands with a boy friend; and Barbie may be dressed
as a bride, a stewardess, a ballerina, or Miss America. Or
the child may be given a mop, a tiny jewel box, a lipstick.
For older girls, there are games: "The Mystery Date
Game," "The Bride Game," "What Shall I Wear?" So much
for the New Feminism.

Many feminists maintain that these toys are forced upon
reluctant housewives by a Diabolical Industrial Conspiracy. In actuality, the toys satisfy certain deep needs—not

the child's, but the mother's. In producing these toys, manufacturers are assuring the mother of her own femininity. They are telling her that the life style she has chosen is the right one and that she is also right in attempting to impose it on her child. If daughter is rebellious, then clearly something is wrong with daughter, who will be hauled off to a minister, doctor, therapist, or, in extreme cases, directly to a mental clinic. In these latter instances, the explanation may sometimes be that mother is so uncertain of her own values that she is unable to tolerate any threat and responds viciously when she is challenged. Mothers also boost each others' sagging egos by banding together to condemn deviance among their children's playmates; and vicious as the young may be to each other, the mothers may be worse. The girl who does not possess the proper toys and the proper attitudes toward those toys will be perceived as the fallen woman of the kindergarten set, and her mother will be credited accordingly.

None of this helps the child. Even the youngest of children has a distinct personality, demanding acknowledgement in its own right. When a child wakes to the fact that she is perceived as abnormal, she cannot help but nurture a special set of guilts and anxieties of her own. As the mother observes these, she sees them as additional evidence of the child's maladaption, and too often she responds by intensifying whatever conditioning she's been attempting already. Deviant patterns tend to harden into rebellion, and many of these rebels will grow up to enter graduate school, if only for lack of any better idea of what to do.

One such rebel is Circe, the eternal enchantress. She is usually an attractive child, and her mother is preoccupied with that single quality. Sometimes, as with Miss Haversham and her adopted daughter Estella in Dickens' *Great Expectations*, the mother's exploitation of the daughter's beauty is clearly and simply vengeful. (Jilted at the altar, Miss Haversham has trained Estella to attract men—and painfully to rebuff them, thus taking vicarious revenge for the shame of her own young womanhood.) Sometimes, as with the stage mother of *Gypsy*, the mother sees the child as extending and fulfilling her own thwarted ambitions. There also can be a note of poorly concealed hostility, if the mother did not want children, especially girls who, in their charm and youth, remind her that she is aging toward death.

Whatever the motivation, Circe learns several things. She learns that her purpose in life is to be lovely and to attract men. But she also learns that attracting a man has left her mother thoroughly dissatisfied. She learns too that it is perfectly permissible to use people as means to some personal end—her mother is manipulative in her handling of Circe, who vaguely senses that she is merely a tool in some maternal game, and Circe herself is taught to be manipulative in her use of her own beauty. In fact, Circe may well learn that she will never get her own way through any other technique. For Circe, as a mere pawn, is frequently frustrated. If she wants a drum, she gets a violin, for violins are more feminine; if she prefers green dresses, she is clad in poisonous pink for much the same reason. If Circe evidences a preference for books or basketballs, she may bring down a storm on her uncomprehending head.

She begins to look closely at the techniques by which mother gets her own way. The woman who is manipulative as a mother probably behaves in much the same way as a wife. Circe quickly perceives that father seldom knows where mother has been, what she has purchased, and how much anything has cost. On those occasions when mother misguidedly tells the truth, there are household storms; when mother lies, the household is serene. Circe witnesses another form of prevarication when mother, who has been screeching like a banshee throughout an intolerably long afternoon, suddenly emerges—gowned, made-up, docile, and seductive—at the sound of father's key in the door. All women's magazines have recommended the technique, without mentioning its probable effects on the moral sense of perceptive offspring.

Having learned the value of deception, she learns elsewhere, unfortunately, that deception and prevarication are wrong, even sinful. In Sunday school and in the family—even on children's television programs—she hears that sincerity and honesty are the basic American virtues, at least technically. Given the right kind of Sunday school she may begin to have nightmares, dreaming that she and her mother are roasting in hell throughout eternity. But she cannot give up the games she knows, even if she is damned for them. Half-consciously, she may already realize that she can use mother's games to escape mother's fate.

When she learns to be coyly seductive, which happens by the age of three or four, she learns, too, to be guilty about this. Having watched mother flirt, she herself vamps Uncle Harry. Uncle Harry buys her candy, and everyone else praises her "cute" behavior. In fact, the entire family breathes a collective sigh of relief, for everyone knows that "cute" girls have no problems. Yet her flirtatiousness inevitably leads to a bad scene. Perhaps she flirts too often with Uncle Harry who, having just finished his third gin and tonic, runs his hand up her skirt and makes her promise not to tell—which informs her that something is wrong. Or mother sees and has hysterics. Or mother warns her several times too often about dirty old men loitering outside the playground and becomes overly preoccupied with the threat of rape. One way or another, she will learn to see her own sexuality as dirty. Thus she dislikes herself. At the same time she learns to despise men—half of them are so weak as to be easily manipulated and the other half are potential rapists. And she does not like women much either. She imagines all of them to resemble her mother, whom she faintly resents. Yet because her outward behavior is normal, her problems will still be overlooked.

Not so Medea. Young Medea is often the product of cross-breeding between a pipsqueak and a dormouse, although her parents may be otherwise lucid human beings who waited too long for a child, who had trouble breeding one, or who are in some other way hypnotized by the mystique of childbearing. Or she may be the child of a woman who has morally—and verbally—armed herself against the evils of husbands, lovers, repairmen, and salesmen. In some way, even as a baby, she learns that aggressiveness will gain her control over weak or threatening elements in her environment.

Thus in infancy she perfects the temper tantrum as an art form, her parents obligingly bribing her whenever she threatens to run emotionally amok. Analyst Leopold Stein seems to believe that every child needs a measure of frustration at this stage. It is necessary for the child to learn that, although he feels the illusion of power, his targets remain "calm and unhurt." The child who is allowed to believe in his own power is "indeed dangerous, both to herself and to others." [14] Medea, unfortunately, never learns this lesson, nor does she learn that tantrums are an unlikely way to obtain the affection she craves. The illusion of power is all she has, and it will still be all she has forty years later when she bellows at her colleagues in the history department.

Gradually, however, she supplements her tantrums with more sophisticated techniques. Observing that her family is wearying, she tries the power of positive assertion. With her chin up and fire in her eyes, she registers her demands. Her parents say "How cute"; and her father insists that she be allowed her way, "just this once." Naturally, a son in the family is punished for this kind of behavior, leaving the boy indescribably confused about the adult world and with serious doubts as to the general worth of the female sex. But little Medea once again sees that she has a good thing going.

Being oriented toward power, she identifies with her father, who seems to have more of it. Desperately, mother gives her baby dolls for Christmas; hopelessly, she watches as Medea bashes their little skulls against the wall. The family therapist mutters about penis envy; but as Clara Thompson has observed, cultural elements are sufficient in themselves to explain what Medea is experiencing.[15] Medea has simply observed that men get their own way with much less trouble and considerably less expenditure of emotional energy. Having tasted power, she will never settle for feminine weakness. Yet all she consciously realizes is that she wants to be something other than what she is. So she escalates her demands, which is all she knows how to do.

Equally unlovable is Medusa, who is not an attractive child. Cold parents or tactless relatives have made her feel this way, even in infancy. Like little Deborah Blau in Hannah Green's *I Never Promised You a Rose Garden*, she quickly realizes that she is not at all what her parents had in mind. They wanted a princess, Jewish or otherwise. Her mother tries to cheer her up by explaining that she will get prettier as she grows up. Like most children, she has no real sense of time or change; and what she hears serves merely to confirm her lurking suspicions that right now she is pretty much of a mess. She is puzzled by the baby dolls and bride dolls that are forced upon her; she envies the dolls' prettiness; but they represent a world to which she has no perceptible way of relating.

As quickly as she can learn to read, she retreats into the world of books. Later she will steal them from her parents' bookshelves, reading beneath the covers with a flashlight; or, in the absence of books in the home, she will shoplift magazines and paperbacks from the corner drugstore. Even when she cannot understand half the words, the pictures draw her out of her own unhappy existence. But her interest disturbs her mother, who may forbid her to read, fearing that she will injure her eyes or that she will be even more poorly adjusted when she enters school. If mother is enlightened, she will encourage Medusa to envision a career or a vocation—something that can begin as a hobby even now—but few women have that breadth of vision. More likely, one of Medusa's few safety valves will be shut at the very time when others should be opened, and there will be an even more stringent attempt to force Medusa to behave like a "normal" girl.

So Medusa squirms, accepting her own guilt. If she cannot stand dolls and habitually leaves them in the driveway to be run over, this obviously reflects a basic flaw in her character. Gradually, she begins to rely on "accidents" as an unconscious defensive technique. Hauled off to dancing lessons—"It can't make her any *more* clumsy," says mother, tactfully—she falls over her own feet, accidentally chipping her partner's brand new tooth in the process. Accidentally too, she sets fire to her new party dress and is forced to stay home; she runs a temperature on the day of the class play. Like Deborah Blau, she may eventually opt out altogether, ending in an institution. At best, making a virtue of necessity, she will learn ostentatiously to reject a world that seems to have no place for her. Unless mother is on guard, her clothes will be held together with safety pins; she will slouch, and her face will sag into ugly lines. These reflect her inner misery, but only Medusa knows that. Her family and friends assume they symptomize her ill-nature and treat her accordingly, which does little to solve the child's problems.

An infant reject from the social order, Medusa may turn brittle or caustic in her defensiveness and this, in turn, increases the difficulty of her social adjustment. Overcome by a sense of the unutterable hopelessness of it all, she secretly examines herself in mirrors and store windows, wondering why she alone in the world was born flawed. With any bad luck at all, too, she will have a Candid Relative who confides to her mother in a stage whisper: "It's probably just as well she's bookish. With that face, she'll never catch a husband." Ostensibly submissive, Medusa retreats to her room to sob her heart out. She is a little young yet to think of suicide. That will come later, when she enters school and her playmates—whose world vision is more reminiscent of *Lord of the Flies* than of the Noble Savage—begin to throw rocks, real and symbolic, at her, figuring that is the sort of behavior she seems to expect. By then, unless she can qualify as class clown, she is destined to descend to the bottom of the pecking order, a position to which she will have become accustomed by the time she begins her professional career.

By contrast, Hebe would seem to have no problems at all. She is simply the victim of her parents' marriage. Sometimes, mother would have preferred to work; her husband believes he would lose status—or attention—if his wife were to take a job. Guilt-ridden because of her own discontent, mother has been atoning ever since, usually by slavish devotion to her husband. Father, thus indulged, becomes spoiled. Or, like most humans, he is insecure; he begins to invent exotic dishes to be cooked or errands to be run, simply because he can prove in this way that his wife still loves him. His wife, in turn, is delighted to be a partner in this transaction, for she has nothing more to offer him although she dare not admit, even to herself, that her affection for him has died as a result of her own frustrations. Whatever the relationship at the beginning of the marriage, the father, by the time Hebe is growing up, is completely ego-involved in these assertions of power by which he affirms his masculinity. That the relationship is more appropriate to a cocker spaniel and its master escapes the attention of both partners, partly because they do not talk to each other very much any more.

Obviously, after a while, Hebe's mother has no way to

communicate her own needs. Even the faintest self-asser-
tion will be perceived as palace revolution. Since everyone
needs to talk to someone, she will occasionally confide in
little Hebe, all the while insisting that the sacrifice is
worthwhile, as Hebe will learn when she grows up. Hebe
privately wonders why. Clearly, her mother's life ended
with her marriage, whatever mother may say to the contrary. And so Hebe rejects the notion of marriage. Unfortunately, she does not also reject the habit of self-denigra-
tion. Indeed, she hardly realizes men are human; she perceives her father as an It, not as Thou. She will continue
to relate to men in that way, and, with bad luck, she will
also carry a heavy burden of guilt. If she had not been
born, mother might have escaped her marriage; she is to
blame, then, for her mother's unhappiness. Often enough,
a parent will point this out to a child, if the child has failed
to observe it on her own. Thus she will grow up with two
habits of thought. She must serve, and she must atone for
her own existence. Teaching may be a way to do both.

Penelope's problems are also well disguised. Either a
fecund or a feminist parent produces Penelope who is en-
veloped, from infancy, in a gynocentric world-view. At
eighteen months she is coolly watching mother breast-feed
the next infant. If mother is a feminist, she finds herself
flat on the floor, examining her mother's body with particular attention to those parts once considered to be private. With mother's full approval, she pretends to nurse
her baby doll at her own flat chest; and she demonstrably
likes dolls, so everyone assumes she's becoming well-ad-
justed. Granted, some of her imaginary games chill the
blood of her playmates' parents: Delivery Room, Organic
Gardening for Good Prenatal Care, Husband and Wife

The neighbors know that Penelope is below the age of comprehension, but they are still scared to leave her alone in the house with their sons. For that matter, the boys are scared, too, which is one of the reasons she may end up in graduate school. Another is the vitality which causes her to take an interest in everything from knitting to football. No one sees that as a problem—yet.

3

In the Schoolroom

In a whimsical, quasi-utopian novel, written at the turn of this century, Samuel Butler prophesized the course of twentieth-century education. Higgs, protagonist of *Erewhon Revisited,* is a guest at the Provincial Deformatory at Fairmead in the country of Erewhon. At the deformatory, he discovers, children are trained to rid themselves of embarrassing virtues. The headmaster explains:

We have to obey instructions from the Grand Council of Education at Bridgeford, and they have established these institutions in consequence of the [Erewhonian deity's] having said that we should aim at promoting the greatest happiness of the greatest number. This, no doubt, is a sound principle, and the greatest number are by nature somewhat dull, conceited, and unscrupulous. They do not like those who are quick, unassuming, and sincere. . . .[1]

Naturally, the "quick, unassuming, and sincere" are to be

deformed in the name of social adjustment. Something very much like this happens to girls in American schools.

For a certain type of girl, feminist texts and teachers would have little effect, nor can conventional stereotyping in the classroom do much more damage than has already been done. By kindergarten, she is an embryonic conformist. Eager to imitate her mother, she is simply marking time until she can marry, sometimes at 15 or 16. In later years, gossiping at the beauty shop or discount house or drugstore soda fountain, such women recall only their boy friends or their proms. Even then they knew the rest was irrelevant. At most, they planned to finish high school or to attend business college for a term or two.

At the other extreme is the woman whose self-assurance and intellectual capacities have been well-developed in the home, so that she is virtually immunized against the social pressures exerted by teachers and schoolmates. Margaret Mead is clearly such a woman. Product of a feminist mother and a careerist grandmother, her experiences in high school are only hazily recalled as "a theatrical performance in which I had a role to play and had to find actors to take the other parts." [2] Similarly, her family background seems to have immunized Agnes de Mille, who had managed to put her educational experiences completely out of her mind by the time she wrote *Speak to Me, Dance With Me*.[3]

Most girls fall between these extremes. For them, the school years can be a time of horror. Eleanor Roosevelt, uncertain of herself, recalled her first school experiences as a time "of agony and mortification," [4] while school curbed Marilyn Monroe's natural vitality,[5] and Hildegard Knef recalls teachers who seemed, in retrospect, to be

sadistic Nazis.[6] Similarly, in Shulman's *Memoirs of an Ex-
Prom Queen*, the heroine's real education comes as a result
of books given to her by her father. In literature she was
able to "forget I was a piece of meat." [7] The process is reversed in college. Through her own naïveté and a male
professor's sexual irresponsibility, a genuine interest in intellectual history is subverted into a tawdry sexual affair,
an exercise in professorial ego gratification. Sylvia Plath,
in *The Bell Jar*, stands out against the system: "I did
everything well enough and got all A's, and by the time
I made it to college nobody could stop me." [8] That she is
exceptional, of course, is in part a cause of her later breakdown. When a girl achieves and feels no shame about it,
she courts disaster. And, at any rate, it is emotionally tax-
ing for a girl to pit herself alone against the world of
adults.

For these women, education is distortion. As Matina
Horner has shown, the girl must be taught to surrender
her ambition and to frustrate her own talent by disguising
her intelligence and "abdicating from competition in the
outside world." [9] In another recent study, Grace K. Baruch
has shown that, even in the fifth grade, a sampling of middle or upper middle-class girls, from whose ranks professional women might be expected to emerge, envisioned
their futures as secretaries, teachers, nurses, actresses,
singers, or stewardesses. While none looked forward to being a wife or mother, few dared to voice ambitions that
would be considered eccentric in a girl.[10]

Part of the problem, of course, is that schools are run
by the most conservative element in any community—professional men. Since women were first allowed into the
school room, men have set the ground rules and done much

of the testing and grading. Characteristically, when Ober-
lin College first benevolently opened its doors to women
early in the nineteenth century, it expected that women
students would wait on male students at table and would
do their laundry.[11] It was assumed, by that generation and
several that followed, that women were forbidden the
"nobler avenues of intellectual distinction," not by men
but by "Nature's stern decree." [12] According to Dr. Edward
Clarke of Harvard, writing in 1873, "higher education was
destroying the reproductive functions of American women,
by overworking them at a critical time in their physiologi-
cal development." [13]

These Victorians trained the professors who trained the
professors who now command departments and colleges
of education. The student clientele of education departments may be mostly female, but its professors remain
male. Inevitably, some are those chinless types whose self-
esteem is defined by their God-given superiority over
women, but many are merely lecturing mindlessly from
notes copied from lectures by students of Professor Clarke
and his ilk. Significantly, Phi Delta Kappa, an important
education honorary, remains closed to women, as of this
writing. Said one of its representatives, lecturing to a
markedly unappreciative class of feminists: "It is out of
the question that women should want the responsibility of
participating in decision-making groups such as ours." Unwittingly, of course, he was echoing the Victorian belief
that women's duty was "unquestioning obedience to law
and orthodox religion," whatever the orthodoxy of the
moment.[14]

Certainly, potential achievers are discouraged by a process as unsubtle as it may be accidental. In the heyday of

the mini-skirt, supervisors of student teachers were known to assign grades according to how high the trainee's skirt was above her knee. A professor of business administration prefaced his course with the announcement: "In all my years of teaching, no woman has ever passed this course. I see no reason that this situation should change." In the creative arts, a young professor is supposed to have discouraged girl students by such comments as: "Well, I guess we gotta look at the work our piece of ass has done." At one Midwestern college, a professor of educational administration habitually announces: "Women should leave this class. There won't be any jobs for women in this field." Since academic grading and hiring are based on the principle that the same person may serve as judge, jury, and executioner—the same man who announces his prejudices then assigns grades, with which no one is allowed to tamper, based on those prejudices and next writes letters of recommendation based on those grades—the girl students are well advised to take the hint. Bright and vital students, their sensibilities outraged, leave the high-status fields for more hospitable, if less significant disciplines. The conformists, the submissive, the masochistic, or, occasionally, the messianic, drop back from prestigious administration programs into programs leading toward classroom teaching.

The conformists, the submissive, and the masochistic survive, and, still smiling, go forth to spread their own values among the young. By the time they are certified as teachers, they have also learned certain modes of survival. One, naturally, is to refuse to take oneself or one's profession at all seriously, so that the teacher is perpetually apologizing for her own professional existence, to other teachers, to parents, and even in front of students. She lets it be known that she will work only until she marries: "It's so important for a wife to stay home." Or until she has her first baby. Or until she earns enough money to help with the down-payment on a house. Or all of these, in sequence, so that twenty years later she is still apologizing for her "temporary" employment, now justified by the need to help her own children through college. Even the recent wave of feminism has had little impact, for, except in the anonymity of large cities, teachers too frequently disdain feminism or fear for their own reputations should they be associated with known radicals. (Recently, for example, a 65-year-old fellow graduate student took the author to lunch in the small Iowa town where she had taught for thirty years. "Don't offer me a cigarette," she whispered. "In all these years, I haven't dared let anyone here know I smoke.") Nor can feminists do much with teachers who are teaching only because their mothers told them to if they were unable to get married, or because they did not think they were bright enough to do anything else, or because they had "a B.A. and no typing skills." [15]

School boards, ofcourse, love these women. They will not make waves. With any luck, their turnover will be rapid, so that the woman hired for a pittance can be replaced for a pittance—and the rapid turnover used as an excuse for low female salaries. Even if the woman should linger for a decade or so, she will never conceptualize herself as a professional, so she will not demand professional salaries or merit pay. It will never occur to her that she might become a school principal. But what may be good for a school board may work to the disadvantage of young girls at the age when they need vigorous and challenging role-models.

A passive and conformist teacher encourages similar qualities in the girls she instructs, especially since it makes her task easier in overcrowded classrooms. "Neatness, conformity, docility," write Nancy Frazier and Myrna Sadker in *Sexism in School and Society*—these are the qualities for which girls receive good grades, although these attributes have little to do with "active intellectual curiosity, analytic problem solving, and the ability to cope with challenging material." [16] A number of other writers have reached similar conclusions—for example, Betty Levy in "Do Schools Sell Girls Short?" and Pauline S. Sears and David Feldman in "Teacher Interactions with Boys and with Girls." [17] Unknown to herself, the child relinquishes the courage that it takes to face new problems, as well as the liberty and individual choice that are part of the American ethos—for men.[18] The teacher, of course, has something to gain. The child's acceptance of her values serves as "proof" that her own life is "right." To question the patterns she encourages in the child would be to question her own existence, and few adults willingly indulge in that kind of introspection.

Moreover, as many feminist writers have shown, the teacher is abetted by the publisher. Texts are to teachers what toys are to mothers—evidence that society approves of their values, as well as ammunition to be used against the child who threatens to deviate. The Women on Words and Images Task Force of New Jersey NOW has examined 134 books published by 14 major firms—a total of 2760 stories. The ratio of boy-centered to girl-centered stories

was 5 to 2; the ratio of male to female biographies 6 to 1.
Of 67 stories in which one sex demeaned the other, 65 were
directed against girls; only three works showed employed
mothers.[19] Elizabeth Fisher found that even when animals
and machines are personified, they are represented as male,
while Marsha Federbush finds sexism, unlikely as it may
seem, in school math texts.[20] In an essay in *College English*, Alleen Pace Nilsen long ago observed that "where the
boy does all of everything and the girl isn't even visible,"
little is being done to help the girl child find a sense of her
own identity.[21] And the problems will be even more severe
for the girl who has found an identity—one absolutely in-
compatible with the stereotypes urged on her by teachers
and texts. Deviance will be punished with increasing se-
verity. One woman, now a professor of literature, recalls:
"As a child, I was driven to school in a car pool. One day,
the driver was the mother of a little boy in my third-grade
class. She asked her son what he got on his spelling quiz.
He said, truthfully, a B. As a matter of courtesy, she asked
how I did. Innocently, I said A. So we stopped at my
house and she waited while I was punished for having hu-
miliated her son in front of his other friends."

Only one option is available. The girl may look to the
role-model provided by the teacher who proves her professional commitment by tacitly disproving her competence at anything earthier. Since her school board assumes
that, at the drop of a zipper, she would flee the classroom
for the dubious delights of housewifery, she sets out to
display herself as unmarriageable. Tending toward man-
nish or dowdy clothes and often indeed remaining single,
this woman herself, as Cynthia Epstein observes, assumes
that the "traits required of a professional woman and those

required of a feminine woman" are "mutually exclusive." [22] There are fewer of these women today; fewer school boards prohibit the employment of pregnant women; and rules barring married women were abandoned long ago. Where she exists, however, she provides an unfortunate example. She is often bitterly unhappy, and her existence suggests to the child that choice of a career means the sacrifice of joy and light and love; and few children are emotionally prepared to accept that alternative.

Relatively few men teach in the elementary schools. By clever coincidence, then, the girl first experiences men as teachers at the time when her conflicts with her family are greatest and when her own sexual turmoil may border on the lunatic. At this point, the male teacher may inadvertently do considerable damage. Men sometimes enter teaching for strange reasons, and in the 1960's many entered to avoid the draft. Among them were decent men of high principles. But others fled from fear, just as, for generations, some few have entered teaching to escape the competition of industry. Competition may be bad. The draft may be bad. Nevertheless, when a man experiences fear, or when he is accused of having done so, he is apt to emerge with lingering doubts as to his own virility. Moreover, he may reassure himself of his masculinity by lording it over his female students. He plays father; he gives orders.

For the bright, eccentric girl who is too involved in her own problems to perceive his, he exerts a powerful force. Because of the nature of his own difficulties, he urges her to accept the submissive role of a woman. By this time, she is probably incapable of going in that direction, but he succeeds in increasing her guilt and in heightening her anxiety. For the girl who might yet go either way, he may well succeed as a father figure. Imagining herself to be in love with this classroom deity, she becomes a "good girl." Unfortunately, in the future she will expect the same god-like perfection of the men she works with and, worst of all, of the man she marries. Needless to say, her disillusionment will be great. On the other hand, if the high-school teacher is a failure at his game, their relationship will degenerate into a mild, harmless flirtation. Parents and school boards being what they are, the teacher will probably avoid actual sexual involvement. The girl, of course, is unaware of these inhibiting forces, and she will be poorly prepared for the reactions evoked by her flirtations later on.

Problems are intensified when the girl enters the intensely chauvinistic world of the college professor. Female teachers exist, but they are usually relegated to the lower ranks, and many until recently had little choice but to grovel before their male peers. Their example was not particularly edifying, and they could offer little help to the troubled student, especially at the graduate level. Moreover, sororities, clubs, and the college dating system have reinforced the view that the university exists for the gratification of the male ego. In the classroom, the woman student is dependent on the tolerance of the male professor. Should he decide she should marry, should he decide that she is too "pushy" to enter his graduate program, she will be flunked out, and she knows she will find no defenders. Similarly, in the life of the sorority, she must put her work aside rather than turn down a date. It is conveyed to her in many ways that her social status is more important than her preparation of a major paper or her performance on a final exam. Moreover, even when she is free, she must not stay up too late studying, lest eyestrain give her a wrinkled look.

Certain rules of the game resemble those that she learned in high school, but there are subtle differences. Probably no one has warned her of them. Many college professors, for example, are more than willing to take young students as sexual partners. Others suspect something is wrong with the notion, but they still yield when they approach middle age. A most frequent and pathetic college phenomenon is the lost young woman who seeks out a graying professor as a father figure. From previous experience—with a high-school teacher, a minister, a relative—she sees him as a source of consolation and advice. On the other hand, he believes she wants to seduce him— it has become terribly important to him to prove that he is still desirable. Whatever happens, whether the girl yields or runs screaming, she has experienced a shock and she has been told once again to define herself according to her sexual function.

Much the same thing happens when the girl is flirtatious. In high school, girls might vie with each other for the teacher's attention, but of course the unstated rule is that the teacher never fully responds. In college he may respond. Too often the girl feels compelled to follow through with what she obviously began—the professor may remind her that it was all her idea—and she finds herself enmeshed in a complex relationship long before she is emotionally able to handle it.

Such problems as these mingle with a multitude of others. The few girls who have not yet learned their places now find that there is no room for them in most of the professions. If the girl needs work, she must be content to make the coffee and carry the mail, while the better-paying student jobs go to the men. Until recently, she could only stand helplessly by, while scholarship funds were granted mostly to men and while some professors unabashedly made a practice of giving women lower grades. It is not surprising that many bright women still see no reason to attend college and that many more drop out, even from graduate school. It has been shown that the drop-out rate is substantially high, even among women rated as excellent by their professors.[23] Naturally, though, the drop-out rate has traditionally been used as evidence of feminine inferiority or instability.

Of the women caricatured here, only Circe is fully prepared to cope with the system—and, unfortunately, for reasons that will adversely affect her future professional and intellectual life. From the time Circe entered school, she studied how to manipulate the male. As a first grader, she watched Miss America pageants; by adolescence, she was shoplifting cosmetics and beauty magazines. She quickly learned that outspoken women—Medea, for example—are objects of ridicule, barely tolerated by their parents, so she settles into the appearance of passivity. The boys make fun of Medusa's tousled and unwashed hair, so Circe's own hair becomes a shining cap. Medusa is laughably clumsy, so Circe practices delicate gestures in front of a mirror. While she may not be beautiful, she can make herself lovely, her childish face frozen into an expressionless, feminine mask.

For the duration of her school years, she will use that mask to manipulate her teachers, just as she early learned to exploit father and Uncle Harry. Grades come easily to her, for men like to believe that lovely girls are invariably intelligent, while women teachers encourage such perfectly socialized little girls. She takes the grades unprotestingly. Secretly, however, she believes herself to be a sham. Eventually, no one will be able to convince her that she is actually intelligent, even in graduate school by which time her intelligence may have ripened. Even then, because she has carefully protected her "virtue," she may assume that her professors are keeping her around only because they want to have another try at her. Unfortunately, this too will be partly true.

By now her sexual nature will be deeply troubled. Warned as a child against sex, she will have grown more skeptical as she watches the fumblings and terrors of her little friends. She knows it is possible to manipulate so as to avoid sexual encounters, and she finds this safer. If she can afford to, she may affect heavy cosmetics and designer clothes, which serve the dual purpose of attracting men and, simultaneously, functioning as a kind of armor. She will be too faultless to be touched. She is the "Ice Maiden," as Karl Shapiro describes her in his academic novel, *Edsel*.

In her college years, she may discover a sense of vocation. Psychology will offer her a way to understand herself, religion her rationalizations for sexual coldness, and literature escape. But in graduate school she must make a crucial choice. If she continues to retreat into her elegant and polished self, she may survive her course work, but she will crumble when she is expected to teach freshman classes. Facing a classroom of squirming and moderately hostile young, she panics. They are expecting a theatrical performance, and they will obviously not settle for a passive vision of female loveliness. Intimidated by the challenge, she may vanish before she finishes her dissertation. On the other hand, if her instinct for survival is strong and if her only perceptible alternative is marriage, she strengthens her will, turns cynical, and masquerades as an extrovert. She flirts with her students—it is, after all, the only technique she knows—and she develops a lecture technique from a study of Sarah Bernhardt and Mrs. Siddons. After all, rhetorical flamboyance is easily come by. Women score high in verbal skills and Circe, at any rate, has spent much of her time alone with the words in her books. Moreover, once she realizes it, verbal fluency is another valuable defense mechanism. Her graduate professors are amused at how rapidly she develops a certain flair, a style. They would be amazed if they knew why.

But she does not talk. Certainly not to them. Probably not to anyone. Isolated, she remains a vehicle for professorial sexual fantasies—those late afternoon reveries in darkened offices for which professors, of all professionals, have so much time. Circe may only vaguely suspect what is going on. She will be puzzled by a passing remark or a totally unexpected sexual overture. Unwittingly, she has become a perambulatory Rorschach test. In turn, the professors' wistful surmises as to her sexual exploits become the gossip of academic parties, most of which would have long ago died, were there not females whose credentials, personalities, or reputations could be served up with the hors d'oeuvres. (The result of one Midwestern party was that a professor, one of the guests, visited a friend of Circe's the next day to ask whether she was actually taking pay from townspeople for her favors.) Thus, while Circe imagines herself to be manipulative, which she is, she is also becoming something of a victim.

Medusa, of course, was a victim from the start, for her imitation of conventional femininity is little short of parody. Observing that other girls smile, she fixes a rigid grin on her face, while her eyes dart about searching for the approval that never comes. Just as her schoolmates torment her, so her teachers, repulsed by the seemingly abnormal, offer her little protection, although one may occasionally call her mother to recommend a dermatologist or psychiatrist. The child naturally hears of all this and her insecurity is increased—not only do people not like her, but they are trying to do things to her behind her back. She resents a world that operates in this fashion, but, still internalizing her guilt, she then feels conscience-stricken by her own hostility. One professional woman, now approaching 40, recalls: "I went around for years feeling guilty. I thought I started the Second World War. The night before Pearl Harbor, I'd prayed that my parents and my kindergarten teacher would all get killed, although I wasn't too sure what getting killed meant. Then the next day the war started. I guess I must have thought that God overreacted."

Teachers, taking Medusa at the general evaluation, put her to work scrubbing blackboards. The women who teach her in elementary school, however, pity her, and their pity takes the form of good grades, no matter what her performance. Realizing that Medusa can never grace a bridal gown, they have not the heart to deprive her of academic awards, too. Unwittingly, they provide Medusa with an out. The child knows that beauty is the important thing, but she will go after whatever rewards she can get. Nonetheless, she will be afraid to announce her new-found interest in chemistry sets. It will be only one more thing for people to laugh at, and her life is already punctuated by her incessant "I'm sorry" and "Excuse me." Studying in her room at night, she becomes good at whatever she sets her mind to, but she will devalue precisely those things she is good at. Years later, she will still be saying: "I'm sorry, I haven't any children—I'm only a microbiologist," or "No, I've only had three Fulbrights." In high school or college she may be a compulsive eater. The rest of the time she runs errands for her professors, babysits with their children, and, in graduate school, does research that will be published under the professor's name. Her teachers still pity her. They give her high grades, but they like to think they are being generous in doing so. By now she may be as intellectually able as anyone around, but the professors cannot convince themselves that ugly girls are sometimes bright. Medusa is content to serve. For the first time she feels useful, and she can escape social problems by hibernating in the library or the lab. Unlike Circe, she cannot escape into her own ego, for Medusa's ego is pretty much of a mess, and she is trying to avoid coming to terms with it.

Medusa's fantasies may include being martyred as a missionary. Sometimes, though, her dreams disturb her. Like Kurt Weill's "Pirate Jenny," she occasionally dreams of a world in which men are slain at her feet—by her command. In college, she may ask for professional help, but she will not get it. Counsellors, mostly male, will shrug her off by telling her it is normal for women to think of suffering. Privately, they will be convinced that her problem is her ugliness and slovenliness, which they rarely realize is the mere symptom of some graver disorder. What it comes down to is that male counsellors do not like to work with ugly women either. Wisely, Medusa decides to pay no more attention to her dreams than she must. Awakened by them, she returns to her lab at midnight to check the food trays for her rats or to take the rectal temperatures of her iguanas. To brood would be to allow her problems to overwhelm her. Then she might do something silly, like drop out of school to live with a cabdriver who beats her. Some women do.

Hebe, too, is badly troubled in ways that too easily can be shrugged off as part of woman's "innate" masochism. In grade school, she is discovered in a broom closet with a prepubescent lecher who convinced her he "needed" her. Her teachers, although they try to ignore grade-school sexuality—it embarrasses them and upsets parents—nonetheless are vaguely distressed. Hebe seems to be carrying conventional femininity to outrageous extremes, and they hazily sense that her behavior is a mockery of their own. Discomfited by the child, the teachers do not like her; they give her high grades to get her out of their classes. (Thus later, however shredded her life, she will cling to academe, for in the past it has provided her with some faint semblance of approval.) It is assumed that Hebe's childish excesses will take care of themselves.

They will not. Hebe's rejection of her mother's domestic servitude takes the form of service to the entire world instead. In another and tamer age, she would have settled for being a nurse or social worker. Now she wants to run away to serve the Indians, the Chicanos, or any oppressed group—though she may not have the faintest idea where to find them. By high school she is choosing boys of other races to sleep with. She may or may not find sexual satisfaction, but the boys are almost invariably left feeling degraded. She could not explain it, and neither could they, but the boys sense that they are being used. In fact, they are Hebe's penance for her existence, and few young men like to regard themselves as a sort of sexual emetic. Hebe, oblivious, may rise to new heights. Since she has heard all Jews are rich, it will not be hard to convince her to run guns for the Arabs. Since drug pushers are among the oppressed minorities, she may be persuaded to run heroin.

Not being stupid, she may avoid being caught, at least until her junior or senior year of high school. At that point, the high school would rather graduate her than expel her, and she will drift from high school to the college. Inevitably, if she is caught after this, the parents and the community will place the blame for her behavior on the college. A Pre-Raphaelite figure, her long face half-hidden by her mane of hair, she lurks in the student union, when she is not taking pass-fail courses in social sciences or human-services or herself rendering service to the suffering multitudes. She rather enjoys college. No one keeps an eye on her, and curriculum and students alike teem with suffering of a type usually bowdlerized in high school. From the death of Keats to the decay of the Incas, all is grist for her intellectual mill. Then, too, young students suffering sexual deprivation need her help. And male professors, so they assure her, suffer too.

Her intelligence and her ministrations get her by. Her professors, who oscillate between sleeping with her and pitying her, contemptuously drop assistantship money in her lap. It is a way of satisfying their own uneasy consciences, and they never dream that she will survive to compete with their boys for jobs. She will have problems, of course. A paper will be late, for she has spent the night rescuing a drug freak from the police. Her disorderly life plays havoc with her health, and she sleeps through exams. So she will be attracted to fields where grades do not count for much and where professors look kindly at that antic behavior in which they themselves indulge. A few older, battered female professors may look at Hebe and sigh, but they have no way to approach her. She would not listen to them if they did.

Of the lot, Medea is most successful. Like her parents, her teachers have consistently yielded to her demands. While they resent her as a deviant and a trouble-maker, they have little time for argument with any individual student. Medea is conscious of their resentment. But she has no way of knowing that it is a consequence of any action of her own. Increasingly, as she grows up, she is preoccupied with her own needs and demands and with techniques of obtaining what she wants. She has no sensitivity to the responses of the needs of others, whom she perceives merely as potential obstacles between herself and her goals. Most women, of course, learn the art of dispassionate demand. However, they learn the method much later in life, and consequently they do not take themselves quite so seriously. Not so Medea. Since the world proves so gloriously submissive, she increasingly believes in her own power, her own rightness. If, once or twice, her statements are so skewed as to demand correction, whatever tantrums ensue—"But, teacher, Bacon wrote Shakespeare! I know he did!"—she will next time prepare her facts. A competent scholar can be nurtured in this manner.

The tendency of the adults in her world to avoid confrontation with her is damaging. What Medea craves is approval. She wants to be a person in her own right, and she is dissatisfied with the powerlessness of women. Instead of working with her, however, teachers isolate her further by putting her in charge of tutoring younger children or keeping the class in order when teacher is away from the room. When Medea is praised, it is for her active —even hyperactive—participation in class discussions. She will later be more than surprised when she finds that this participation is no longer welcome in college. She also directs the school play. All of this makes her more and more of a loner.

By high school or college, two distinct gifts have been developed—inadvertently, of course. First, Medea possesses and exploits a certain facility for verbal tyranny, and, second, she is serious-minded. Her social relationships are troublesome, but she has two escape routes. She may retreat, like Medusa, into some field of proficiency, from whence she can take potshots at girls who are more facilely socialized. Later, she will similarly attack younger and more attractive colleagues. Or she may deliberately cultivate flirtatious mannerisms, though the result may be clumsily unconvincing. She is oblivious to real sexuality, of course, for she is incapable of the selflessness of orgasm, but she knows sex games can be played for raw power. Besides, she likes to watch her teachers hyperventilate. Her sexual intransigence, like Circe's artfully arranged eyes, may well produce grades and even assistantships where more straightforward measures have failed. The balding, pot-bellied professor, whose homelife is a saga of frustrations, aids Circe because he still has hopes. He helps Medea because she reminds him of his wife or his mother-in-law, and he has never won an argument with that kind of woman in his life.

Surprisingly, Medea marries quickly. Marriage is still a mark of the status that she craves, and it is easy to excavate a shy biologist or a timid librarian from the dark recesses of any campus. He stands by, faintly bleating, while she continues her education—which after a while he may encourage, just to get her out of the house. She will rarely be approached by any other man. The intelligent and sensitive intuit the drive for power that underlies her behavior. The majority, neither sensitive nor intelligent, are perceptive enough to fear the unleashing of her tongue. When she marries, she has provided herself with an explanation of why men so often avoid her. What is more, marriage provides her with a defense against critics. Males and females alike, she assumes, are jealous of the woman who seems to have everything—intelligence, marriage, and, eventually, children and a Ph.D. Thus, freed from any further need to take others into account even occasionally, she can finally cross that line separating the outspoken woman from the holy terror.

Offhand, Penelope would seem least likely to pursue an academic career. In high school she is president of the Home Ec Club. She is a cheerleader. She is the life of the party. If she is troubled at all, a male teacher is more than happy to play father figure, with the possible repercussions noted earlier. True, when she delivers a lecture on natural childbirth to her brownie scout pack, she scares her little friends and their mothers out of their uniforms. True, too, that in high school she seldom dates the same boy twice. But adults love her. They assure her that a husband will come along. Of course, someone may hint that marriage and child-bearing involve complex relationships with men—getting them, talking with them, and, sometimes, hanging on to them. Penelope is not prepared to admit this. Being female is enough. Should she have thought about the matter at all, she will have concluded that men are intended to remain figures in the background, providing help, consolation, wisdom, and wealth when the need arises. It will never have occurred to her that men are more human than this, rightfully having needs and desires that might conflict with her own.

Since husbands are not hard to acquire, she frequently does marry. This keeps her out of circulation until she has exhausted garden clubs, bridge, women's golf associations, community service, and her husband's patience. In one little Midwestern university town, bored housewives and faculty wives had formed a six-month waiting list for a chance to do volunteer work at a local hospital. While waiting, they kept two therapists in business and, according to one local store manager, accounted for the major portion of local shoplifting. Eventually, her wearied husband suggests she take some classes "just for fun." This, of course, is often a path to divorce. One 45-year-old mother of six began with a few courses and ended, divorced, as a faculty member at a prestigious Western institution; while another, who began work in English "just for fun," soon packed up her four children, divorced her husband, and left for a career in social work in the East.

These situations presuppose an already foundering marriage. Under more stable conditions, the wife will continue taking courses. Often, she simply does what is required—little more, little less; there is sometimes a peculiar, dull quality to the student who is also a housewife. But even dullards get degrees. Sometimes, if a graduate chairman or department head is having problems with his own jealous wife, dullards who are also dowdy will receive a large percentage of whatever assistantship money is awarded to women at all.

Sometimes Penelope remains single. Entering graduate school, she begins to find companionship among other women. They compare notes—about their families, their sex lives, and the chauvinism they have encountered. Penelope has always enjoyed being biologically female. Now she finds she would enjoy it more, if it were not for men. Her frustration increases as she nears the end of her graduate work, for, at about this point, professors begin to take her aside. They ask why she does not marry. They do not understand why she wants to take jobs away from the males who are also graduating. Of course, once there was no one who placed more faith in marriage than did Penelope. Now, in her real sense of frustration, she is enraged. Frequently, she is radicalized and longs, just once, to kick a senior professor squarely in the groin. She begins to itemize past grievances and she finds they are numerous. She may become a lesbian, at least for a while. By the time she finishes graduate school, she is still dutifully smiling at male professors—after all, she has little choice if she wants her degree. Secretly, though, she is ready to pick up a placard and march on something—anything.

Part Two
The Rigged Match

4

Men, Manners, and Gamesmanship in Academe

Whatever a woman's problems as a student, she will have perceived most of them as personal and peculiar—unless, within the past few years, she has become involved with those radical feminists who find chauvinism underlying everything. Usually, serious awareness of bias develops only when the woman, near completion of her graduate work, begins to search for a job. After all, as a student she shared her subordinate position with others of both sexes. All alike deferred to experienced or distinguished professors, and most found passivity to be the better part of valor. Only as she interviews for jobs does she develop a more jaundiced view of her chosen trade. This, her first real disillusionment, will be followed rapidly by others. With some shock, she perceives herself as a player in a game for which no one has taught her the rules, rules that are not only unspoken but often unspeakable. Depending on the early development of her personality, her reaction will range from depression and self-doubt on the one hand to anger on the other. Of 84 women interviewed for an American Studies survey, 38 responded that "rage" best described their initial reaction to academic chauvinism.[1]

Forced to reassess the academic game, the woman will discover what many critics of higher education have been repeating for years. But graduate students are rarely encouraged to read these critics, and their conclusions, at any rate, look slightly different from a woman's point of view.

1. Ph.D.'s Exist for the Purpose of Producing Other Ph.D.'s

Universities, so the myth goes, are communities of scholars, and scholars are those who add to the body of human wisdom, who conserve the wisdom of the past, and who are immune to the methods and motives that contaminate business and industry. With the possible exception of some instructors in agriculture, business, and the R.O.T.C., in fact, professors exist in a virtual ecstasy of moral and intellectual fervor. This is because, so the myth continues, universities attempt to retain the traditions of the Middle Ages, when scholars lectured freely (only a few of them being denounced or burned) to docile and respectful students (only a minority of whom rioted in the towns) who had no control of content or curricula (although their professors were sometimes paid by the head). The doctorate, it is assumed, is the crowning glory of this ancient system, and present requirements, though seemingly lunatic, would be meaningful if only the callous, ignoble, and insufficiently intelligent students of the mid-twentieth century were intellectually capable of appreciating this great tradition.

Actually, universities of the past were delightfully sloppy. Wealth could purchase degrees, and even spying for a monarch, as Christopher Marlowe may have learned, sufficed for the waiving of requirements. Instructors might be dilettantes, as was the Rev. John Stevens Henslow, whose dabblings in botany, entomology, chemistry, mineralogy, and geology—in idle moments stolen from his principal studies of theology and mathematics—were sufficient to qualify him as a Fellow of the Geological Society and a leading candidate for a Cambridge professorship of mineralogy.[2] Until the 1850's, Oxford and Cambridge had not formally accredited scientific curricula, and the doctoral degree, as we know it, did not exist for them. Too, in literary studies, the English tradition of journalism and belles-lettres gave way to the academic article only in the nineteenth century. Early scholars wrote for a less specialized audience. Trained as a Fleet Street journalist, George Saintsbury, for example, resisted throughout his career the obscurities of the new-fangled academicians, the encroachments of organized research, and the "kind of fact-grubber who could get excited about whether Chaucer had been taken prisoner near Rennes or near Rheims."[3] There had always been fact-grubbers, of course, especially in such fields as classics which had increasingly narrowed into the study of historical linguistics. These fact-grubbers invented their own great traditions, resisting changing knowledge and changing times—their arguments against the introduction of science and of English literature into the curriculum were almost precisely those used today against black, feminist, and cross-disciplinary studies—and, mostly, the fact-grubbers lost.

For whatever its illusions, the university cannot exist in isolation from the world outside. In fact, it can be argued that the American university, as it developed, was altogether too sensitive to its milieu, being profoundly influenced by the values of the modern industrial complex with which its development was chronologically contemporaneous. It has been remarked that, as late as 1880, there were less than a dozen professors of history in this country, and even these were expected to branch out into such subjects as logic, literature, and moral philosophy. But there was little room for the Renaissance man amidst the specialized, technological development of the late nineteenth century; and academics, not to be left out, sought to emphasize their own kinds of technical know-how, the American Historical Association and the Modern Language Association both springing into existence in the 1880's to be followed, in short order, by many others. Growth, competition, specialization—these values also were absorbed from the Mauve Decade and the Gilded Age, and the lesson was well learned. As Ben Morreale has remarked: "No other industry has had such a phenomenal rise in job productivity since 1900, expect perhaps advertising." [4]

Amidst the snobbishness of those glittering decades, it became necessary, too, for professors to find a way to distinguish themselves from those masses, including women and blacks, who were becoming permanently entrenched in the lower echelons of education. Although, as Don Cameron Allen has observed, only four of the first MLA papers were "scholarly," the rest being pedagogical in nature,[5] there was soon a noticeable shift toward "research," its techniques imported from Germany, that other nineteenth-century center of industrialization. The wide-ranging Anglo-French intellectual tradition was sacrificed to narrow Germanic specialization, probably, or so one suspects, because this new kind of fact-grubbing gave the illusion of technological exactitude in an age that valued just that, and not much else. The notion of the research degree was developed. Since then, while academic research, despite its own best efforts, still occasionally contributes to knowledge, it has tended to remain apart from the intellectual currents of the times. From Freud, Darwin, and Marx to T. S. Eliot, Einstein, and Picasso, seminal materials have continued to emerge in the world outside, to be exploited, or more commonly resisted, by American academicians.

More important to the status of women in academe, professors themselves have remained incoherent as to exactly what it is they are doing. Many scientists deny that research is possible among philosophers and artists. Certain historians and literary scholars, on the other hand, vaguely suggest that reading books is research enough. They see no need for publication, and they have no great respect for the kind of research that happens in scientific laboratories. The one point on which all agree is that research gives status, as classroom teaching does not. Yet research alone will not buy the groceries. Professor Allen cautions that, while a professor's scholarly work may keep him alive intellectually, "he should never forget that society keeps him physically alive because he is a teacher." [6]

But what can researchers teach, without being mistaken for hirelings of the lower orders? Obviously, researchers can teach research.

Obviously, too, this will lead directly to a superfluous number of Ph.D.'s who will in turn insist upon producing Ph.D.'s of their own, for they will naturally crave the status of their mentors. Logically, then, certain of the warm bodies needed to fill the graduate schools should be discouraged from seeking employment, in an attempt to hold down the proliferation of Ph.D.'s and Ph.D. programs. Thus, in the recent past, women who had been admitted to graduate programs were discouraged, as they neared completion, from finishing the dissertation or from seeking employment. To hold back the tide, only males need be encouraged. Moreover, such segregation preserves status, which traditionally diminishes when women enter a field, and it provides a servant class for menial chores—for example, freshman composition and remedial mathematics —and frees researchers for their more prestigious teaching of research, when they teach at all. Again, for those uncertain as to what exactly they are supposed to be doing, it provides a definition of a sort: research, whatever it is, is something that can be done best by white males, with the exception of an occasional eccentric drawn from a wide range of races and sexes. For the socially ambitious, the exclusiveness also suggests a pseudo-aristocratic climate, delicately reminiscent of the joys of Pall Mall or Cavendish Square in some earlier age.

2. Upward Mobility Through Academe

In the absence of any coherent system of values and any clear definition of purpose, one function alone has gone unquestioned: the use of academe for upward social mobility. A 1938 American Association of University Professors survey showed that, of 4667 members of the organization, 26.6 per cent were sons of businessmen, 24.7 of farmers, 12.1 of manual workers, 10.6 of clergymen, 5.1 of teachers, 5.1 of physicians, 4.1 of lawyers, the small number of those remaining being the sons of professors, chemists, engineers, public officials, editors, writers, artists, and musicians.[7] And this was before a new wave of the socially unhousebroken returned from World War II and Korea with the G.I. Bill in hand and before the expansion under industrial and governmental subsidies in the 1950's and 1960's. Even before these last events, however, Logan Wilson perceived that "If one were looking for comparisons in other societies, American academicians would have more points in common socially with the new quasi-proletarian intelligentsia of the U.S.S.R. than with the aristocratically inclined university staffs of pre-Nazi Germany." [8] Commenting on their "philistine style of life," Wilson might more tellingly have compared them with the squabbling *nouveau riche* of Stendhal and Balzac or with the socially ambitious clergymen scrambling through the Barsetshire novels of Anthony Trollope. And it is highly unlikely that women will understand this behavior, for women come from significantly different backgrounds. Helen Astin has shown that 31 per cent of the fathers of academic women hold at least one college degree, as opposed to 7 per cent of the fathers of academic men, these being considerably more likely to have completed only a grammar-school education.[9]

As in suburbia, membership is restricted. Ethnic origin may not be important—within limits. Milton M. Gordon, in "The Intellectual Subsociety," summarizes information gathered concerning 61 college and university professors. He finds that these "intellectuals do in fact interact in patterned ways and that these patterns are largely undelineated by ethnic background." [10] In other words, Albanians and Serbo-Croats need not worry, just as they go unquestioned in most suburban neighborhoods. There also seems to be little anti-Semitism, probably as a result of the impact of Hitler's Germany on doggedly liberal consciences of the 1930's. Racial and sexual differences are another matter. The black and the single woman are still no more welcome than at the suburban country club. In 1958 Theodore Caplow and Reece J. McGee found that "women scholars are not taken seriously and cannot look forward to a normal professional career" and that "discrimination on the basis of race appears to be nearly absolute." [11] Tokenism has done remarkably little to change that situation, and comparisons with suburbia remain unavoidable. For example, on occasion after occasion, a male professor contemplating marriage with a female colleague is taken aside by another male to be warned: "Look, screw her, if you gotta, but don't marry her." While the law may have forced blacks and women into the academic neighborhood, one still does not want to find that one's brother has married one.

Nowhere is the resemblance to suburbia more evident

than at faculty social gatherings, although admittedly these
are more evocative of the Trollopian tea table than of the
alcoholic antics of Westchester County. Young professors,
male or female, waste long hours in anxiety lest some professor or his wife dislike them. Others observe with dislike those academic hustlers who angle for power by inviting the "right people" to a home-cooked meal. Caplow
and McGee note that "the assistant professor who offends
the dean's wife at a party may be as severely punished for
it as the lieutenant who offends the colonel's wife in a
similar situation." [12] That such social trivia can affect a
career plays havoc with the popular notion that pay, tenure, and promotion are based on merit, unless merit be
defined as the memorization of handbooks by Amy Vanderbilt and Emily Post.

And it is obvious that, at any such gathering, the female
professor is as unacceptable as is the widow or divorcee
in the suburbs. At best, she is merely tolerated. Academic
husbands and wives alike believe that women are supposed to be supportive; too often, they also believe that
women are intended to be idle. Inevitably, a woman colleague will have been unsupportive on some professional
occasion, and she is rarely idle—at least, no more so than
are the husbands. The professional woman is imperfect, as
women go. She will be patronized by both husband and
wife, and the wife's judgment, no matter what the subject,
will be taken more seriously than will hers. Obviously, of
course, not all faculty wives are graceless clods. But, to
them, the professional woman can present a peculiar
threat. Faced with a bright woman professor, the wife
feels guilty because she has not developed her own intellectual potential. An attractive professor is clearly a threat

in another way, while even a dumb and dowdy woman may be perceived as a mark against the husband's or department's hiring policy. There is no way to win, so the woman professor retreats into a corner where she pretends a passionate interest in needlepoint and the price of steak. She resembles Balzac's Cousin Bette, skulking in the corner of the Hulot home, dependent upon the good nature of the family in its fleeting moments of interest; and the effect upon her character can be equally unfortunate. Where she really wants to be is in the next room, where the men are gathered, possibly involved in discussing policy matters that will directly affect her. But the wife of the host will have more input into their decisions than she and will know about most of them considerably sooner.

3. The Old Boys Club

Nationally, many of the more traditional disciplines are dominated by another Victorian or Edwardian institution, the old school tie. Involved are tenured professors of Ivy League institutions, spiced by a few Californians, and, in recent years, by select representatives of the Big Ten. Ben Morreale describes how this inner circle looks to an outsider at a convention:

The Down-and-Outer, pale and wearing a thin tie in a green that was popular four or five years ago, is usually alone. . . . He stands at the entrance of the lobby watching the shouting, milling crowd, attaches to his lapel the sticker that tells his name, and the fact that he is from some forgotten college from the upper regions of a state a thousand miles away. He watches a party of graduate school professors enter wearing Abercrombie and Fitch suits, with camel hair coats draped over their shoulders like cloaks. Their faces are tanned and finely grained, shining like hazel nuts, and they shout as they recognize one another.[13]

The young man, standing outside with his nose pressed against the pane, can still dream of being admitted to the club through his scholarly attainments, although this is less likely than many young men suppose. Even an excellent scholarly contribution will not be properly recognized if its writer is unusually young or old or located in a "minor league" school. Nonetheless, he can dream. A woman, looking on the same gathering, cannot.

Chances are that she will not even study with members of this elite. In the past women were far more likely to be admitted to schools with minor-league graduate programs. Thus her professors, too, must reconcile themselves to being perennial outsiders. They have a way to do this —again male-oriented. Returning from their conventions, they build fantasies about their own departments, which, they assume, are meritorious and unrecognized only because of the snobbishness of the Eastern establishment. To again cite *The Academic Marketplace*, Caplow and McGee found that 51 per cent of the department chairmen sampled believed their own departments to be among the top five in the country. The researchers christened this the Aggrandizement Effect, defined as a tendency for groups to "assign unrealistically high ratings to their own groups in comparison with competing groups."[14] It is a game in which any number can play.

Having convinced themselves of their own excellence,

professors rarely caution their students as to the professional worthlessness of many minor-league doctorates. After all, the professors do not want to believe it themselves. Moreover, it would diminish the number of bodies in their classrooms; and, as observed earlier, a research professor cannot survive without embryonic researchers to teach. At graduation, the student often believes his degree to be something it is not, and, as usual, the arrangement is most damaging to the female. If a young man holding a provincial university degree has trouble finding employment, then one can imagine the limitations placed upon a young woman holding the same degree, unless she is in one of the relatively rare fields where token women are desperately needed.

The club system manifests itself on larger campuses in still another way. It isolates the members of various disciplines. Scientists, returning from their conventions sorely stricken with the Aggrandizement Effect, will grumble at money spent on what they consider fifth-rate foreign-language programs, especially when their own excellent operations remain short a dozen diamond knives or a specialist in Mesopotamian treetoads. "Thirty years ago," laments C. P. Snow in *The Two Cultures: And a Second Look,* "the cultures had long ceased to speak to each other: but at least they managed a kind of frozen smile across the gulf. Now the politeness has gone, and they just make faces." [15] It might be added that the faces grow nastier as budgets continue to tighten. When schools are large enough, there is even little social mixing. The half-dozen college psychologists will meet together each and every Saturday night, although they long ago ran out of anything new to say, while their wives, often having nothing whatsoever in common, are driven to adultery, psychiatrists, or, at least, nervous twitchings. Yet the effect on women faculty can be even eerier. If a woman—or black—is isolated within a department, she may try to make friends elsewhere in the institution, and that will be a serious error. If she makes such friends, she is damned for her association with members of departments considered academically inferior. If she makes no such friends, she may end up speaking only to her Siamese cat, except when she is discussing house plants in the corner at faculty parties— or even, as in several instances, babysitting for male colleagues so that the men and their wives can freely socialize together.

4. From Old Boys Club to Fraternity

Within individual departments, especially those large enough to house graduate programs, the old boys syndrome gives way to something more nearly resembling the American fraternity system, whether Lambda Chi, the Masons, or the Moose. Here the tendency is to secure status by placing arbitrary and often irrelevant roadblocks to hinder the professional progress of underlings—roadblocks resembling the hazing of fraternity row or the tribal incantations of Masonic initiations and guaranteed merely to produce a bland and banal conventionality among the survivors.

At the top of the pyramid, naturally, are the research scholars. Some obviously deserve to be there, but the larger number are non-successes fondly imagining themselves to be the inglorious Miltons or Gauguins or Einsteins of academe. They identify themselves as "men of knowledge," their function being to search out knowledge and to correct previous authorities and theories.[16] Some, in fact, do precisely that. Unfortunately, these are off buried in their books. The 24-hour day being what it is, they have not the time to concern themselves with department rituals of tenure, promotion, or cocktails. Frequently slow producers, they are apt to disappear for years at a time.

The larger majority, however, have perfected the art of quick and flimsy publication, being researchers only in the sense that their paper consumption causes shortages at the mills and depletes the forests. Jacques Barzun best describes this academic norm: "One has only to listen to the private confidences of the ablest scientists and scholars and to have oneself some familiarity with a given subject to be persuaded that an enormous amount of the research output in all fields is: (1) repetition in swollen fragments of what was known more compactly and elegantly before; (2) repetition, conscious or not, of new knowledge found by others; (3) repetition of oneself in diverse forms; (4) original worthlessness." [17] Such writings have been called exercises in "professional narcissism." [18] Only infrequently do they raise or answer significant questions or problems of methodology. Nonetheless, aspirants to the higher circles are urged to go off and produce more of the same, while certain less desirable elements of the academic community—women, for example—receive teaching loads so heavy or so geographically scattered as to remove them neatly from the competition.

But production of printed matter is not enough. There has developed, too, a secret language, one more complex than that of teenage street gangs but designed to the same end. Like the argot of the gang or of the ghetto, it is intended to baffle those accustomed to the nuances of normal English; it serves as an artificial barrier against outsiders. Young men working as reading and research assistants are tutored in the language. Blacks and women, it is assumed, are incapable of learning it. Having had relatively infrequent access to those offices in which it is learned, they often handle it more clumsily, finding it difficult to master the jargon in time for quick post-graduate publication.

Even more remote from intellectual activity are those other standards by which the newcomer is frequently measured. In one Midwest university town, the social center was an Elks Club, and it was assumed that all newcomers would join. Not altogether coincidentally, single women and blacks were not admitted; and, the club being located on the upper floor of a building, they could not even yell their contributions to departmental policies through the windows. Then, too, there is clothing. Lewis Coser has observed that the "denizens of faculty clubs, even in major universities, have tended to look more and more like the men one encounters in the executive cafeterias of major corporations." [19] "I always thought Professor —— was bright," said one ambitious young man of a senior colleague whose several thoughtful books had been highly praised by a discriminate few. "But I just noticed, he never shines his shoes." The young man is now a prestigious figure in his field. He knew what counts. Needless to say, though, the woman who adopts the tailored style will be gossiped about as a "lesbian," although the woman who adopts any more feminine style will be regarded as "too frivolous to be a good scholar." Even the levis and workshirts affected by certain social scientists are a uniform, of a sort—and one strikingly unbecoming to many middle-aged women professors, and repugnant to many blacks.

Other inner circle phenomena include secret societies, charitable committees, and dining arrangements.[20] These may range from the private and often sexually segregated clubs of the Eastern establishment to their lowly Midwestern equivalent—the stealthy telephone calls leading to private luncheon meetings in a local bar. For that matter, even bad manners can be a status symbol. Protected by rank and tenure, senior men may revert to the proletarian gaucheries of a misguided youth. "This is where we'd have the party if you were faculty," said an English professor, leading a parade of teaching assistants through his living room. "But you're grad students, so we'll go to the basement." Marital status, too, enters in, as in the business community. In a survey of social scientists published in 1958, Lazarsfeld and Thielens discovered that 1972 were married, 396 single, 36 widowed, and 40 divorced.[21] However prevalent divorce has since become, many women still find it advisable to lie about their marital records, lest a known divorce lead to questions as to their emotional stability.

Newcomers, all of them demonstrably insecure, are well advised to imitate where they can. And, among them, there will be a hustler, for the system encourages the man "who studies the professors, doping out the easy graders, the likes and dislikes of this or that man, the opportunity for jobs, until he emerges with a Ph.D. which he looks upon as a union card to enter a wider field of imperial exploitation." [22] Not only does he imitate the old guard, he sets new hurdles before the young. He organizes Sunday football, unless there are young blacks in the department, in which case he organizes soccer or rugby or something else at which they are unlikely to be proficient. Needless to say, women colleagues, when notified at all, are urged to sit on the sidelines with the wives, which puts them in their place. If many of his immediate competitors are single, he arranges gourmet dinners among couples, so that each wife in turn prepares a meal—and the single person becomes the outsider.

Shunning such controversial matters as politics, he concentrates upon activities that are (1) conventional and banal, and (2) those at which he excels. Before long, he will be spotted as an organizer, a bright young man, and a hand will reach down from the stratosphere to guide him into some plush appointment—undergraduate advisor, for example, or chairman of a library or research committee—where he will have no rivals and where his promotion and tenure are virtually insured. From that vantage point, he will systematically eliminate the remaining competition. Still an instructor or assistant professor, he has access to the more youthful social circles, where he will study weaknesses or, at least, collect gossip that can be used to terminate some promising career. Trusted by his superiors, he will be able to spread his information where it will do the most good. Thus the hustler's values are perpetrated, and his competitors never quite realize what happened to them.

5. The Hustler Mentality and Academic Freedom

Few have been so naïve as to assume that the academy has ever been a bastion of intellectual freedom. Many professors, returning from the Second World War with the hope of enjoying their recollections in tranquility found instead the era of the McCarthy hearings. By the same principle of aggrandizement noted earlier, each individual evidently assumed that he himself was important enough to be threatened, and the result was a perceptible timidity. Certainly, in the late 1950's, a significant number of academics evidenced concern lest their political beliefs be distorted, while even more were anxious lest they be subject to community gossip.

But the problem lies deeper than this, as Lazarsfeld and Thielens suggest when they observe that political anxiety seems to spill over into fear of "*any* kind of unconventionality," a theme more recently repeated in the academic repudiation of even the most harmless manifestations of counter-culture and student freakishness.[23] Not all can be blamed on McCarthy. Self-interest is as rampant in the academic community as anywhere else, partly for lack of any other clear-cut standards. Some of the academic hirelings who met student protests with the argument that the university should remain detached from politics were, at the same time, subsidized to invent new nerve gasses and the like. They are little different from the Louisiana professors of the late 1930's who, according to a perplexed Bertrand Russell, "all thought well of Huey Long, on the ground that he had raised their salaries." [24]

For academics are so accustomed to self-censorship that it takes little to acclimate them to similar pressures from outside. They themselves have eliminated certain materials, especially those involving sex and women, from the conventional curricula for years and have exerted certain other equally unsavory pressures. On a campus where divorced women are not hired, a woman lying about her marital record will nervously delete "sensitive" materials from her sex-and-marriage course. Her timidity may be reprehensible, but no more so than the prejudices that force her to that point. The conventional mores of the academic community even influence curriculum in such unworldly fields as literature. On a campus where homosexuals are fired—as still happens—it is highly unlikely that a male teacher will present a full and sympathetic treatment of, say, Oscar Wilde or Lytton Strachey. If he is single, he probably will not treat such figures at all; neither would he dare write about them. Where heterosexual activity is not allowed as a subject of discussion, the professor may turn to the expurgated texts of Shakespeare, still reprinted, at least as late as the 1969 publication of *Dr. Bowdler's Legacy*, by both Oxford and Cambridge University presses.[25]

And, in academic publishing, anything having to do with sex or women ranks low in prestige, and young scholars are urged to plough the traditional ruts. Thus in the 1971 *PMLA Bibliography*, some 150 articles and books on Chaucer are listed as having been produced in a single year—not to mention almost 500 papers and books on Shakespeare produced in that year. Yet the most hackneyed work on one of these figures has been considered more prestigious than the rediscovery of some previously lost woman writer; and apart from Emily Dickinson, Jane Austen, and the Brontës, women writers have gone as unnoticed in academic journals as they have in most college classrooms. And something like this is true of most academic disciplines.

Even the least radical of women, then, is apt to notice that she has spent much time and energy training for a job in which she will not be welcome, amidst colleagues whose values are unconsciously designed to cripple her. Her Ph.D., she discovers, has been a lengthy and expensive exercise in what Jacques Barzun has fittingly termed "preposterism." But by this time it is far too late to start over. She is too old. She is too well trained for any other "female" work, as employment agencies will be quick to tell her. Besides, she may possess a genuine dedication to her subject or to her students. And many remain as a function of messianic fervor, figuring that higher education is too important to be left in the hands of men who, in the name of objectivity and academic freedom, are willing to expunge the records and negate the efforts of a large portion of the human race. So the woman settles in, as best she can.

5

Below the Belt and into the Kidneys: Rites of Passage

Before examining the ways in which troubled women interact with the frequently capricious, biased, and even mindless male inhabitants of the academic community to produce situations that are emotionally volatile and legally complex, it is necessary to examine more closely the ways in which women enter the academic community. Their initiation rites oddly complement normal academic gamesmanship without being quite part of it, for one simple reason: most male candidates are exempted from playing such games.

The process of being interviewed and hired is fraught with peculiarities enough to shatter the nerves of the sanest and best balanced of female characters, let alone Circe or Medea or Hebe. Mercifully, however, many women until recently have remained at least partly oblivious to what was happening. The woman whose experiences in the job market were little short of catastrophic would write them off as unusual, providing that she later attained tenure and promotion with relative ease or that she was psychologically prepared to accept a lifelong assistant professorship. After all, she found a job, did she not? Similarly, the rare woman candidate who had been encouraged to conceptualize herself as authentically professional—the gently nourished product of a fastidious graduate school —would regard her later disasters as peculiar to the intellectual backwater in which she unaccountably—she thought—had found herself. Only in recent years have most women become conscious of any pattern. On the other hand, the woman who experiences nothing but misery and who, after the first interview, forsees the future as little more than a depressingly grim continuation of her graduate-school woes may well leave the profession altogether, often without bothering to complete her dissertation. And all, thanks to earlier conditioning, experience moments when they suspect that what has happened to them is either woman's fate or woman's fault—and their male friends are quick to reassure them of this.

Of recent years, though, many women have compared notes, compiling a substantial pool of genuine horror stories. There is little research into these horrors, their surrealism defying statistical survey and analysis. But the anecdotes below represent actual experiences gleaned from the recollections of women who are, with one exception, still active in the profession. Neither are these the rationalizations of failure, for, again with a single exception, the women involved have achieved relative success. In fact, Helen Astin has observed that it is the women who are most active professionally and who publish frequently who are most likely to report employer discrimination, their unusual aggressiveness, frankness, or competitiveness accounting apparently for their greater productivity and their greater willingness to voice their complaints.[1] And perhaps these very traits also account for the greater amount of hostility evoked in the males who are threatened by them.

1. Preparing a Dossier

Normal academic routine dictates that, somewhere between the preliminary doctoral examination or its equivalent and the completion of the dissertation, the student will establish a credential file, either in the office of his graduate chairman or in the placement office of the college or university from which he will graduate. The graduate adviser may or may not offer his help. Most frequently, individual professors look after those students, usually male, who have worked individually with them as research or reading assistants. Even a woman's own dissertation adviser may be slightly startled and generally uncooperative when he learns that she actually intends to compete with men for jobs. (One of Caroline Bird's respondents believes that, in large metropolitan centers, a horde of women Ph.D.'s is encouraged because, kept unemployed, they can be hired privately and cheaply to do "assisting and research scutwork—the intellectual slave labor on which so much academic work is based." [2] In some cases, when he realizes the candidate is serious in her effort to find work, the adviser seems actually to put new obstacles, albeit unconsciously, between her and the completion of the dissertation, demanding a new chapter here or a new graph there. A woman can assure herself of competent advice only by carefully timing a sexual liaison with a senior professor, arranging for him to weary of her at about the time she is prepared to graduate. The sexual relation will guarantee his attention; his boredom will inspire him to find her a job, preferably in a far distant city. But the delicate timing is not easily managed, and few women are ever advised to handle matters in this way. Besides, most women do not want to.

More often, the female candidate blindly follows the male model. She borrows a copy of vitae from a fellow graduate student and thoughtlessly copies what she sees there, or she is honest in filling out the standardized forms that many colleges demand. She assumes, mistakenly, that she should list the same information that the male includes. This is simply not so.

First, there is evidence that a woman's personal life, especially her marital status, "is considered a relevant factor in her application, although clearly it is not relevant in the consideration of male applicants." [3] For a man, it matters little whether he is married or single, provided that a limp-wristed single middle-aged man is not also a specialist in notoriously homosexual poets. For a woman, it is a substantial advantage to be single, unless she is so ill-advised as to be widowed, separated, or divorced. The married woman is assumed to be subject to her husband's whims, goals, and job mobility. The widow, it is assumed, is biding her time until her next husband. The separated woman will dart back to her husband whenever he beckons. The divorcee, so the myth goes, is (1) promiscuous, probably with students (*Playboy* magazine recently reported a study of 150 professors at San Francisco State

University, of whom 40 said they had experienced a sexual affair with a student and another 40 said that they might—but it is somehow different when a woman does it[4]), and (2) emotionally disturbed. For practical purposes, then, the man might as well tell the truth, for it can do him little harm. The widowed, divorced, or separated woman should list herself as single, which is technically true. The married woman should try to avoid giving any information at all.

Worst of all, many women honestly acknowledge the existence of their children. For a man, children are hostages to fortune and ensure a stable employment pattern. For a woman, naturally, it is otherwise. Unless the children are grown—in which case she will be considered too old to begin a career—it will be assumed that she will skip class at every sniffle and will disappear completely at the first symptom of the mumps. Fortunately, even standardized forms do not ask how many children a woman has given birth to. If anything, they ask how many she *has*. Some sensible women have taken advantage of this and have temporarily given over custody of their children to a benevolent aunt or sympathetic parent, thus allowing them to evade the issue with as much honesty as can reasonably be expected under the circumstances. But these women have usually been advised by a wise senior professor, and most departments do not have senior women who are willing to involve themselves in such delicate matters of advisement.

Along with marital status, the student is expected to list previous work experience. Many graduate students, especially those in education and business programs, have had prior teaching experience in the high schools. This can count in a man's favor, especially if it were only a stopgap measure to avoid the draft in the 1960's. For a woman, listing the experience is another mistake. Her work will be perceived as evidence, if any is needed, that she is a teacher, not a scholar, and that she should be placated with a section of freshman composition or something remedial. Similarly, she should avoid listing the frenetic employment by which she has earned tuition—jobs as barmaid and go-go girl are highly suspect, and experience as secretary will be taken as evidence of a second-rate mind, or worse. Too, both men and women may have been away from school for a number of years. The man may safely list his army experience and even, in such wild-eyed fields as sociology, a year spent cruising the Amazon in a rowboat ("It makes him seem *so* interesting"), but the woman had best weasel around those years she spent raising children. Likewise, only men may safely list community activities. Masons are safe almost anywhere, and some administrators warm to the thought of a Rotarian, Rotarians being highly unlikely to carry picket signs or to start S.D.S. groups. Not so with the P.T.A. or the League of Women Voters, which will be regarded as proof of the candidate's "feminine" unprofessionalism.

2. Letters of Recommendation

While the woman is systematically bungling her vitae form, she will also be soliciting letters of recommendation, which are generally far more important than almost anything else. For the well-known scholar's students, jobs can be arranged far in advance by an opportunely placed memo to a friend. In *The Academic Marketplace,* Caplow and McGee note that, while academic recruitment is theoretically open, in practice it is "mostly closed." [5] Ben Morreale realistically observes that good jobs are awarded in advance, adequate positions are sent along the professional grapevine, and what is left over put up for grabs to the "intellectual longshoremen." [6] Logan Wilson explains this as the desire to "avoid being flooded with applications from unqualified persons," noting that, in an investigation of a typical middle-ranked university, four-fifths of all appointments were handled through some form of grapevine.[7] But there is a problem more serious than mere administrative laziness. Even now, when Affirmative Action programs are forcing advertisement of positions, many chairmen, after scrutinizing (presumably) countless applications from women and blacks, still find cause to hire the white male students whose names are circulated through an old boys network.

Unaware of the grapevine in some cases and unable to tap into it in most others, the woman candidate usually requests run-of-the-mill letters, Xeroxed to be circulated from a single typed copy. Naturally, the candidate cannot know what is in the letters. Most gentlemen's agreements in academe are flouted with the greatest of (occasionally illegal) ease, but this particular conspiracy of silence remains sacred. Since the letters will follow an individual around for the rest of his life, the shrewd candidate, sensing disaster after an interview or two, will contact a friend at another school and ask that the friend fake a request on official stationery for the candidate's file. Women rarely sense when something is going wrong (since their female friends' interviews so seldom go right, they have few standards for comparison); neither do they usually have good enough advice or strong enough friendships to get away with this tactic.

Moreover, a woman may not even know who is to be avoided in requesting letters. A seemingly benign professorial countenance may mask a dyed-in-the-wool chauvinist who has smiled at her only because she is cute or because he is too timid to state his views publicly. In his letters he may well play the snickering, leering buffoon or he may vent decades of previously stifled spleen at women who venture to compete with him for jobs. This sometimes happens to men, for obviously quite different reasons, but the probability is greater that a woman will be routinely and efficiently sabotaged.

The problem is compounded by academic timidity. In his book on *Male Chauvinism*, Michael Korda writes that, in business, men "will cheerfully fire a man, with a minimum of fuss and guilt, while in conveying bad news of any kind to a woman they will invariably assign the responsibility to someone else. . . ." [8] The academic community includes many sensitive souls in full flight from the brutalities of business and industry. Few academic men want to confront anything at all, and they want to confront women less than that. Consequently, the male graduate student whose career was endangered at some point will have only a fuzzy sense that something went wrong, and the woman will know nothing at all. Alike, they may puzzle over failing grades, and they may sense that the grades had nothing to do with any similar curve in their own performances, but all this is nebulous and most graduate students know better than to ask questions. Thus real problems are often concealed only to emerge in letters that the candidate never sees. And so, years later when the woman manages to see her file, she is horrified to observe that three letters deal with problems of which she was never aware, while the fourth is a vituperative and vindictive epistolary masterpiece, having less to do with her than with the professor's turbulent marriage or his homosexual loathing of the female species.

Circe, for example, may request a letter from a man with whom she has been flirting. No more than that. The middle-aged professor, in fact, may be a trifle resentful that she is escaping the department with the relationship still unconsummated. His letter will read something like this.

Dear Professor Pecksniff:

At the request of Miss Circe Veneering, I am writing to recommend her for a position in your history department. I am sure she will be an asset. She is bright, cheerful, and relates well with students, especially the men. Decorative, she also mixes well at large parties.

Her dissertation, I believe, is written on a woman of the French revolutionary period, but I can assure you she is no feminist. As yet, I have not found occasion to examine her dissertation, although I am a member of her committee. As you know, John Tallboy, about whom I wrote you earlier, is finishing a dissertation under my direction at this time, and I have been preoccupied with his work. I am sure I have told you that I think his study will be a substantial contribution to knowledge of eighteenth-century agriculture. Nevertheless, I can assure you that Miss Veneering's work has always been quite adequate and her prose style readable. She seems splendidly adjusted as a woman, and I have no reservations in recommending her for your teaching staff.

Nancy Jo Hoffman, in her study of "Sexism in Letters of Recommendation" (from which certain phrases in the letter above have been bodily lifted), writes that "the rare comment on a male's appearance is simply a footnote, the frequent comment on a female's, a thesis statement," [9] and Circe, unwittingly, has virtually asked for treatment of somewhat this sort. Whatever the quality of her work, she will be preceded by certain types of letters which insure that she will be viewed as a teacher, not a scholar, and as a decorative frill, useful for flattering male egos so long as the college budget provides for such fripperies.

Circe's polar opposite, Medea, will likewise be damned with faint praise. Her letter, though, will read something like this:

Dear Professor Chuzzlewit:

You asked at the last conference if we had any likely looking candidates in classics. As you know, it's hardly a popular field these days, but we do have a woman, at least, who'll graduate this spring. Her reputation as a scholar is quite good; she's already published two brief papers with Professor Necrophile. You will also find that she is absolutely reliable. She never misses a class, she attends every meeting to which graduate students are invited, and she reads, God help her, every memo that comes through the campus mail.

I should warn you, however, that she may be a trifle difficult to work with. While tolerably attractive, she's hardly sociable, and I sometimes find it difficult to distinguish her everyday greetings from hostile professional attacks. She's aggressive for a woman, both intellectually and socially. To be honest, she seems to get on well with her students, but with all the little feminists running around these days one never knows if one is hearing honest reports on women teachers.

The candidate's name, by the way, is Medea Gradgrind. She is married. Her husband is completing his work in biology and also is seeking a job, which may complicate matters. If she proves unsatisfactory, I do have another candidate, a very bright young man who will finish his work in the fall term.

All this assumes, of course, that neither Medea nor Circe are actually regarded with contempt, as poor Medusa may be.

To whom it may concern:

I am writing in support of the recommendation of Medusa Slipslop, who has applied, I am told, for a position in chemistry. Miss Slipslop, despite her unprepossessing exterior—unfortunately, she does not make up in beauty what she may lack in brains—has an excellent reputation as a research assistant. She is industrious, docile, and cooperative. I should think the chances are slim that she will leave her work to marry. Nor can I predict, frankly, a successful career as a researcher. Obviously, she must have experienced great personal difficulties as a woman, and, although there are not yet signs that this has significantly affected her performance, it is a factor that must eventually be taken into account.

Finally, there is the bluntly chauvinistic approach—refreshing, at least, in its candor—of which Penelope is the likely victim:

Dear Professor Barnacle:

Penelope Wombly has asked me to write in support of her application for a position in your English department. Mrs. Wombly is the divorced mother of four and must clearly labor under serious handicaps. (I know nothing about the divorce.) As you will observe, she is an older woman, having recently passed her thirty-sixth birthday. I find it regrettable that she chooses to take time from her children, and that she considers beginning a new career at her age, but that can't be helped.

Considering everything, however, she has been a good student. She has a lively intellectual curiosity, is anxious to please, is willing to relocate, and will probably be grateful for any work you can find for her.

In Professor Hoffman's study, certain patterns are apparent. First, to warrant letters more satisfactory than these, the candidate must be both "chic" and "brilliant," a combination even rarer in the academic world than among the human race at large. But anything less will evoke negative responses. Moreover, as Professor Hoffman observes, the "figurative language" of letters about males suggests that the candidate's career will be "active, linear, progressing through time—from lowly instructor to full professor, from fledgling writer to serious scholar. . . ." The woman's letters, on the other hand, will focus on static qualities—her sensitivity, cooperativeness, warmth, and manners, as well as her rapport with students.[10] The difference reflects Simone de Beauvoir's premise that the male is regarded as transcendent, the female immanent, a "creature of another's will, frustrated in . . . transcendence and deprived of every value." [11]

3. The Slave Market

Unaware of the recommendations that have preceded her, the candidate next signs up for one of the hiring conventions. The nature of these varies considerably, from the vast slave markets of the American Historical Association and the Modern Language Association (although, during the past several years, there has been a serious attempt to bring these chaotic hiring situations under some control) to the smaller regional meetings of the American Philosophical Association and the rather more Dionysian revels of the artists.

In the Apollonian stillness of the MLA, the few women who usually attended (until their miraculous emergence from the academic woodwork in the early 1970's) were extraordinarily visible among a horde of men peculiarly addicted to the IBM style of dress. Before the early 1970's, there were the job seekers and there were the nuns. The latter, neither seeking jobs nor sexually approachable, were the only women who seemed to enjoy themselves, queueing past the book exhibits, listening to the papers, and glorying in their freedom from the convent. The secular female, in her visibility and vulnerability, was forced to operate in a professional straitjacket.

Much information concerning available jobs, for instance, is passed by word of mouth in convention hotel bars. At the more conservative conventions, however, the female job seeker, if she was at all sensible, would avoid the bars where her presence was—and to a lesser extent still is—interpreted as inviting a pickup. Should she strike up a conversation, she might find that a certain reputation had preceded her to the next interview. If she were ugly, she would be christened the Wife of Bath; if pretty, someone would have labeled her the Whore of Babylon. On the other hand, if she avoids the bars, she is deprived of essential information, unless sympathetic male students— unlikely in the face of a depressed academic economy— form an efficient grapevine in her behalf.

The other primary source of information is the book-exhibit hall, where, if her luck holds, she can eavesdrop on a covey of chairmen or encounter an old graduate professor who knows of a new opening. Even the exhibit hall, however, is fraught with hazard. (Reliable rumor has it that, at the 1974 MLA convention, a browsing female scholar was approached by a male professor who mistook her for a publisher's agent. "Hey, gal," called the male, and verbally assaulted the woman when she did not turn to meet his needs. Pressed beyond endurance, she slapped him—so the report goes—and then found herself charged with assault and battery.) Rather than brave such dangers, she may try to wrangle an invitation to a publishers' party, where she will be made more ill-at-ease, even if accompanied by a prominent male scholar (and that is probably the only way she will get in, at all). Publishers bring their own women employees whose duty is to insinuate a sales pitch into their flirtations.

Usually, then, the female applicant is stuck with what interviews she can arrange in advance, a number substantially smaller than those scheduled by males. In 1967 an outstanding woman candidate from a Midwestern school compared the results of her letters of application with those of male candidates, none of whom could equal her academic record. All had sent out some 300 letters. For the men, the letters had evoked courtesy responses ("Sorry, no jobs") from about three-quarters of the schools, expressions of interest from many of the remainder, and about 10 interview appointments. The woman received four requests for interviews; most schools did not even bother with courtesy letters. Lately, Affirmative Action has been the cause of a cruel variation in the game. More schools are scheduling interviews with women, but the individual woman has no way of knowing, although she probably should by now, that the interviews are no more than gestures to ward off governmental investigations. Thus the individual emerges in a state of depression, wondering why she meets no one's standards and fills no one's needs.

At the larger conventions, the interviews themselves are scattered over crippling geographic distances, which works to the disadvantage of the female who is likelier than the male to be judged according to her appearance, an appearance that is in no way improved by a three-hour bus and subway battle. And, for men and women alike, the interviews can be models of discourtesy. In his detective story *Deadly Meeting*, Robert Bernard cleverly caricatures MLA manners, inventing a depressingly life-like chairman who, badly infected with machismo, mocks a candidate into profanity by attacks on his short stature. The chairman, with patently false astonishment, wonders how the candidate can enjoy lecturing: "'I should have thought it might be a bit difficult for you to—well, to be seen by your audience.'" [12] Then, of course, there is the chairman who openly scoffs at a candidate's Semitic nose. Both men and women suffer, but the docile, passive, and sensitive female is least prepared to cope. After one such experience, she may flee the convention altogether, leaving the field wide open to the surviving insensitive clods. One elegant woman, possessing all of Circe's neurotic inhibitions, trudged and subwayed from Manhattan to a motel on Long Island to find her interviewer at the door in jockey shorts, having just risen from a plainly visible bed containing an equally visible naked woman. "C'mon in, honey," called the woman, chewing her gum and shaking her breasts. "I was just gettin' up." She dressed, while the candidate nervously bungled her interview with an obviously bored and sated professor. The candidate kept no other interview appointments and, shortly after, left graduate school to enter a publishing house. From the many versions of this story circulating among women in a variety of disciplines, it may be surmised that this technique has proven to be an effective way of discouraging women, while ostensibly interviewing them.

It takes little imagination, too, to envision Medusa, tapping at a door in Chicago's Palmer House, on her face the pleading, trustful expression of a cornered dormouse.

"Come in," she hears—so she interprets the muttering through the door.

She enters, clumsily catching the door on her foot. The professor does not notice. He is standing in front of a mirror, adjusting his tie.

He allows her to stand and sweat for a few moments. Then, as if startled, he turns. "Why didn't you take a seat?" She wonders how she could have done something wrong already. "Who are you, anyhow?" She had rather thought that he would know.

He fumbles through a stack of manila folders as she gives her name. Opening the file, he manages to look disappointed.

"Victorian literature, eh?" he sighs. She agrees. That was, after all, the field for which his college had advertised an opening.

"What do you know about Ben Jonson?" She fumbles, Jonson being several centuries outside the perimeters of her specialization. "Well, what about medieval lyrics?" She manages to mutter a critical platitude, dimly recalled from some undergraduate survey course. "Well, you wouldn't mind teaching them, would you?" Desperately, she allows that she would teach just about anything.

"We only have an opening for an instructor," he lies. (Three men from her department have been interviewed for assistant professorships.) "And we expect all our faculty to teach a heavy load of freshman composition." (No one had mentioned this, Medusa knows, to any of the men.) "What's more, I won't have anyone fooling with those feminist courses. Not in my department." Anxiously, Medusa swears she would not dream of it, hoping he will not have noticed that her dissertation involves John Stuart Mill.

"I don't suppose you'll go off and get married," he muses. He looks at her. "No, I don't suppose you will. Well, I wish I had more time to talk, but I gotta meet someone. I may be in touch with you."

Demoralized, Medusa rushes to her room to re-emerge, tear-stained, in time for the next interview for which she is in no way psychologically prepared.

Early each year, artists also meet, usually in some smaller city unknown to those more conservative disciplines for which Chicago frequently marks the western boundary of civilization. The spirit of the artists' gathering, too, is rather different. Despite their frequent sexual innuendos, English professors and historians, on the whole, prefer a tone of high moral earnestness or of aristocratic social polish, however unconvincing these veneers may be. Artists, on the other hand, like to believe in their own orgiastic fervor.

Here, such a candidate as Hebe will find herself greeted by a gale of masculine laughter as she knocks at the door of the art department chairman's room. It is six o'clock, and her interview was scheduled at four. She's been knocking at the door at half-hour intervals.

"Hi!" says a glassy-eyed young man, winking at her as the door flies open. "Have some grass."

"Hi!" says Hebe weakly. Under normal circumstances, she could cope, for the young man is clearly a member of the undernourished proletariat. But interviews are supposed to be different. Hebe does not know what to do with a whole roomful of men on whom her future life depends. Stammering, she explains why she is late.

"Oh, hell," says the middle-aged, paunchy chairman, a man clad in levis and a denim shirt. "I guess I forgot. We were at a studio across town, and I guess we stopped for a drink, and Henry here had this idea and . . ."

"I'm terribly sorry," she apologizes, being programmed to believe that, however unlikely, bad scenes are always of the woman's making.

"That's OK," says the chairman benevolently. "Hey, anyone got the box with the interview folders?"

"Naw," says someone. "Guess we forgot to bring it."

"Doesn't matter," giggles a delicate male creature. "This little girl's always got a box with her. Ha! Ha!" Hebe, despite her previous track record, blushes. The men laugh on.

"You're here about a job?" asks someone else.

"Yes."

"I tell you what, luv. This just isn't the time. But you hang around and have some drinks and maybe tomorrow . . ."

Inventing an excuse, Hebe, like Medusa, returns to her room where she bursts into tears.

She need not feel alone. Across the country, at a regional meeting of philosophers, it is an hour later, and the foddered herd is beginning to wander back from dinner. An especially attractive Circe, riding up in an elevator, feels a pair of fingers clutch at her rump. In this fashion, she meets the man who will become her chairman. He asks if she is interested in a job, and he arranges to meet her later in the evening. Jobs being scarce, she agrees. She will accept the job, and, for the next several years, she will experience the consequences of this peculiar mode of hiring.

4. The On-Campus Interview

Despite all odds, some women candidates survive to be invited to a campus or two, where they will be looked over by resident faculty and administrators. These few interviews will usually be with minor-league universities and colleges, for these are the ones that hire women.[13] Comparing what she is offered with the generally more substantial prospects of her male friends, the woman realizes how much is at stake in each interview. Often she works herself into hysteria or something approaching catatonia weeks before the crucial day. In the decades of plush academic living, tension was eased slightly by indulgent travel allowances. Most men and some women would have been flown to the interview and housed in whatever passed locally for a quality motel. Nowadays, of course, the candidate is invited to Volkswagen across the prairie, possibly with reimbursement for gasoline, to be housed on the lumpy mattress in a dormitory or a professor's spare bedroom.

Appearance, at this point, becomes a staggering problem. When Medea brings dowdy clothes, she finds herself patronized by a doggedly sophisticated department. If

Circe dresses fashionably, she finds her prospective colleagues to be fundamentalists of a particularly puritanical bent. Or else the faculty may tend one way and the administrators another. Caplow and McGee report one such situation: "We had one young woman come down here from one of the Big Ten. She had the M.A. and was working on her doctoral dissertation and we would have very much liked to have gotten her, but when she saw the Dean, he turned her down. He didn't like the way she was turned out, thought she was too stylishly dressed. We had thought she looked very lovely." [14]

Having packed the wrong things, the candidate Fiats through the Rockies. Exhausted, she checks into a motel or dormitory, as instructed, and, still obeying orders, she calls the chairman at his home. She expects an invitation to dinner, for her male acquaintances who were interviewed here were dined in the chairman's home and wined later with a party at the Faculty Club. Instead, the chairman encourages her to have a good night's sleep, saying he will pick her up first thing in the morning.

In a dormitory, she dispiritedly goes to her room and broods; at a motel, she bathes, changes clothes, and heads for the dining room. Numbers of professional gentlemen are drinking at the bar. She, too, would like a drink after her long drive, and she orders one. As if something were yet needed to demoralize her, the eyes at the bar begin to gleam. One man leaves the bar to walk by her table, muttering something that, mercifully, she cannot quite hear. She fixes her eyes rigidly on her drink, and prays that none of these men is the department chairman who is to interview her the next day. (In one instance, a local lecher waved two twenties in the face of a woman soon to become his colleague—having looked at everything except her face, he obviously did not recognize her when they later met. She remembered him, quite clearly.) As quickly as possible, she returns to her room.

In the morning, her prospective chairman picks her up at the motel and with minimal civilities—they have never hired many women, he explains—he transports her the several miles to campus. She is taken to an office and placed in a chair. There she sits, while faculty members come by to inspect her, quizzing her mostly on her abilities to teach freshmen. No one asks about her dissertation. Often they do not talk with her at all. They talk at each other about affairs in the Faculty Senate, somewhat startled, in their inbred way, that she is not cognizant of every subtlety of their problem. Finally, someone murmurs: "Well, women aren't really interested . . ." He asks her whether she has found a boy friend.

The afternoon may be spent dancing to the Chauvinist Gavotte, especially at a school where Affirmative Action investigators have been swarming. She will be shuffled from chairman to dean to president or provost, and at least one of the three will insist that, while he himself would love to hire her, she would really be more comfortable somewhere else: "We want to hire women, of course, but —chuckle, chuckle—you'll find your chairman [or whoever is not talking with her] a terrible chauvinist, and— ha! ha!—you know how rough that can be." A variation occurs when one of the three insists that she is not qualified for the job for which she is being interviewed. Pressed to hire women, they have cleverly arranged to invite only the wrong ones, as they later "discover" with a great show of shock. As it turns out, what they really need is a medieval art historian with a Ph.D., while, through some error, they have invited an M.F.A. in ceramics. Or, to replace a senior American Studies man, they have "accidentally" called in an instructor whose specialty is English as a Second Language. There will be profuse apologies. Later, the chairman will smugly announce that he has done all he can—he has looked at some women, but they are simply not as well qualified as the men. Another variation is to make sure that one of the interviewers asks exceedingly offensive questions: "And what method of birth control do you use, my dear?"

Humiliation, though, is usually not enough. The woman may still take the job. In 1971 an ad hoc committee for Women in History reported that only 26 per cent of women, as opposed to 54 per cent of employed men, received more than one job offer,[15] and the situation is not likely to have improved much. The candidate may well be desperate.

She is not alone. In a metropolitan area far across the country, Medea is undergoing another kind of ordeal. She and her husband both took degrees in the same year, assuming that, if he took a position in an urban area, she would be able to find employment at one of the many other colleges. Temporarily humbled, Medea arranges what interviews she can in the city and in towns nearby. (One woman, realizing the only available job would involve 150 miles a day of commuting, suggested to her husband that they live apart during the week. Having never prepared his own meals, he was outraged, seeing nothing amiss in her driving that distance through the throes of a Northern winter, so long as she was home in time to fix supper. She quickly filed for divorce.) Medea's interviews will be with schools worse than her degree and credentials warrant. And the worse the school, the more hallucinatory the experience.

At one school, she is separately interviewed by warring factions. The chairman calls her into his own office to meet his cronies. "We're badly divided, I'm afraid," mourns one. "You'd better be careful whom you associate with. If we can offer you anything." Later, she is interviewed in a coffee room—which such a school usually dignifies with the title "commons room"—by a rather different, shabbier lot. The chairman absents himself from this session, which is spent mostly warning her against the people she met earlier.

At noon she is taken to meet the chairman's wife. "We always have her look over the women, my dear," explains the chairman. "Saves trouble, y'know." Waiting in the chairman's living room, Medea is startled by the emergence of a middle-aged woman dressed in 1950's floozy style, her several layers of sloppily affixed eyelashes and her dyed hair lurid against a too-tight pink cashmere sweater and skirt. Cowed, Medea mumbles: "How do you do." The chairman's wife unsmilingly looks her over from head to foot and announces: "I hope you know we don't drink here. I'm a Mormon."

Lunch, drinkless, is strained. Afterwards Medea is taken back to the coffee room, there to await, alone, the belated arrival of the dean. The afternoon is long and dreary. Few faculty members drop by to chat, and those that do tend to turn the conversation toward the inadequacies of their fellow professors. Dusk falls. A woman enters and begins to chat about the literary theories of Oscar Wilde. Medea relaxes her guard, for this is the first time that anyone has mentioned books all day, despite the fact that this is, presumably, a department of English literature. But she has relaxed too soon. The woman offers to light Medea's cigarette and, in doing so, allows her fingers to caress Medea's arm. The fingers run up and down the candidate's bare flesh as a strange, pleading look comes into the interviewer's eyes. Medea, flabbergasted, chatters frenetically about Oscar Wilde. She is on the verge of hysteria, but she will take the job when it is offered. She has little choice.

But this is not the nadir, which falls to the lot of a married Penelope. Penelope, too, must find a job near her husband's place of employment, but, since Penelope also has several small children, extensive commuting is out of the question. Finding herself in a small, isolated Midwestern town, she has little choice but to write to the chairman of the English department at her husband's school. In return, she receives the following:

Dear Mrs. Hushabye:
While the university has no nepotism clause, I regret that I must inform you that my department has never yet found a position for a faculty wife, and I do not believe that one will be available in the foreseeable future. Should you insist on presenting your credentials, you may leave your papers with my secretary, and, should occasion arise, we will consider you for some freshman composition courses. The salary would be in the vicinity of $1200 a year.

Penelope, of course, collapses. It was not quite for this that she suffered through her doctoral program. Nevertheless, she has only three choices. She may pack up the children and walk out on the marriage—some do. She may convince her husband to look for another job, but, all too frequently, the husband does not even see what she finds offensive about the letter. Or she can beg for the freshman appointment, taking it—if she can get it—with the full knowledge that she will never be considered for a better position. For, as Alice H. Cook has observed, once the faculty wife allows herself to be hired as a menial, she will never be approached by a search committee, and she risks public humiliation if she calls attention to herself: "One young lecturer was told the search committee would first look over outsiders since the department preferred 'new blood' and someone with a 'serious interest in a career.' " [16]

It would be nice if such anecdotes represented exceptional situations. They do not. Thus many women evidence some of the symptoms of battle fatigue by the time they appear on campus to teach their first classes. Too, well-balanced women discover a previously unsuspected ability to hold a grudge, and even the best-natured and sweetest-tempered discover hitherto dormant wells of anger within themselves. For the less stable—Medea, Circe, Hebe, and the like—this initiation period has triggered the worst aspects of those defensive methods developed in childhood. And nothing about the first decade of employment is designed to soothe these people down.

Part Three
The Carnage

6

Chaos in the Classroom and Elsewhere— The Early Years

Unlikely as it may seem, a few women survive to take jobs in prestigious universities. There they live happily ever after. As Cynthia Epstein writes, "when the firm or organization is of high rank and good reputation, it is probably more likely that a woman can expect fair and open treatment than if she were at an institution of lower rank." [1] Besides, a lifetime assistant professorship at Columbia is, on the whole, rather less depressing a prospect than the same permanent rank at a minuscule state teachers college in a hitherto undiscovered area of North Dakota. With clocklike regularity, however, surveys show how few women are absorbed by "good" schools. Patricia Graham, for example, writes that, in 1968–1969, only 11 women were full professors at the University of Chicago, as opposed to 464 men of that rank. Moreover, six of the 11 women were in social work, a traditionally "feminine" field. Similarly, at Columbia University which, according

to Professor Graham, awards doctorates to an exceptionally large number of women, only about 2 per cent of all
full professors were women.[2] True, a greater number of
women are listed at the lower ranks, but statistics of that
type may be tricky, for many of these women may have
been hired as academic cannon fodder.

Most women gravitate to educational Siberias—minor-
league state universities and smaller private institutions.
There, if the institutions are large enough to support research at all, women scientists, at any rate, may make a
good life for themselves, for scientific research is susceptible to some semblance of objective evaluation—at least
more so than is, say, research in the humanities or in history. While there are relatively few women scientists, they
do have a better chance of being judged—eventually—on
what they accomplish than are women in the more neb-
ulously defined and conservative academic disciplines. Of
course, many women scientists do not like the standards
they are judged by, but they are at least likely to know
what those standards are. Pay has remained relatively discriminatory since a decade ago when, shockingly, the
median for men was from $2500 to $3000 more than for
women,[3] but in the early years it is not the pay scale alone
that does most women in. The most serious problems are
those of human relations, insofar as they lead to ill-consid-
ered and biased judgments. Among the sciences and certain of the social sciences—disciplines, for example, involving computer research—tasks are defined, division of
labor is relatively clear, and the results are measurable.
Under those conditions, human relationships apparently
lose some of their complexity.[4] In these tightly disciplined

fields, the most conspicuous problem is the frequent refusal to hire women at all. Caroline Bird cites the example
of Maria Mayer, who was able to enter full-time teaching
only after winning the Nobel Prize for physics in 1963.
Until then she had merely been permitted to work in her
husband's laboratory at the University of Chicago—without pay.[5] Thus it is among the slovenly disciplines—English, education, history, art, sociology, foreign languages,
physical education—with their built-in uncertainties, in-
securities, and nebulous goals that the women who are
hired are subjected, with cavalier abandon, to every un-
pleasantry in the professional repertoire; which is extensive.

A thumbing-through of old AAUP *Bulletins* offers interesting insights into the geographical and professional
locales likely to give rise to problems so severe as to cause
full-scale AAUP investigations. In the winter *Bulletin* of
1968, for instance, there is a report of a dismissal from
Frank Phillips College in Texas of a woman variously employed as (1) assistant librarian, (2) teacher of women's
physical education, and, apparently in her spare time, as
(3) instructor of biology. In 1969 *Bulletins*, cases involving women were reported from Dutchess Community College in New York and at Bloomsburg College in Pennsyl-
vania; both women were employed in the social sciences.
In 1971, apart from the remarkable case of Angela Davis,
dismissed as acting associate professor of philosophy at
UCLA, there were cases involving two instructors and one
assistant professor of English at Grambling College in
Louisiana and an instructor of biology at Tennessee Wes-
leyan College.[6] One looks in vain for women of high rank

and normal academic appointment at major schools. They do not get in trouble largely because they do not often exist.

We will assume, however, that all our women have been hired at moderate-size universities or, at least, at respectable colleges not yet on the brink of bankruptcy. All—even Penelope—have been hired at the rank of instructor or assistant professor—probably the former, except on those campuses that have abolished instructorships altogether. In such subjects as history, women are six times as likely to be hired as instructors or lecturers than are men, and only half as likely to receive assistant professorships.[7] For all, this is the first professional appointment, although a few may have had previous experience as teaching assistants.

Women and men, of course, share equally certain shocks of adjustment. There is nothing discriminatory, for example, about the effect of finding oneself alone in a strange city, helplessly wondering where the gas company has hidden itself, what laundromat is safe from mugging, and where, without learning duplicate bridge, one can go to make contact with others of one's species. Men and women alike are equally resentful to find that the college feels no responsibility, and its faculty no interest, in helping the newcomer with the problems of finding housing. Similarly, all share the shocks of new class preparation. Freshman English, at one school, may be nothing but composition; at another, it may be given over to the mysteries of linguistics or syllogisms or the history of the language, and it is perfectly possible that the new teacher has only the most tangential acquaintance with anything he is now called on to teach. Nor is any new Ph.D. apt to have the slightest acquaintance with teaching methods.

But, as always, the implications are more serious for the woman. In the Astin and Bayer study, "Sex Discrimination in Academe," it was observed that more than two-thirds of women teachers and fewer than half of the men were expected to teach undergraduates almost exclusively, while teaching loads themselves were heavier for women.[8] What this means is that, totally untrained for teaching, the woman must nonetheless stake her professional future on what happens in the classroom. And she will have less time than the man to prepare any single course adequately. To her despair, she realizes that her research degree is virtually worthless and that her graduate education has almost no bearing on her job. Meanwhile, an incompetent male teacher may turn toward publication or administration—or he may continue teaching his courses at the graduate level, maintaining that none of his colleagues is equipped to evaluate his work on such advanced levels.

Desperate, the woman may try for quick publication, but the prospects are grim. She will probably be hired by a university that lacks an adequate research library, and the burden of her five-day-a-week and two evenings of teaching leaves her little time or energy to travel across the state to whatever major university facilities are available. In fact, a schedule that places her in the classroom at 8:30, 10:30, 2:30 and 4:30, with office hours between, may even make it impossible for her to cross town to major libraries in New York or Chicago. Jessie Bernard suggests that it is this crippling of women in terms of the type of place where she may be hired and the work load given her that is responsible for lower productivity among women. Sex is a less important factor since "scientists in universities, whatever their sex, are more productive than those in colleges, whatever their sex" while "women in universities . . . are more productive than men in colleges." [9]

Moreover, there are additional roadblocks. Bitterly, Ben Morreale's Down-and-Outer claims that editors, incapable of discriminating among essays themselves, are dependent upon recommendations from establishment scholars. [10] Probably this is something of an exaggeration, but, as previously observed, many newcomers, especially blacks and women, have not been properly drilled in the professional jargon of their chosen fields, and the quality of jargon too often seems to be more important than the quality of thought. Moreover, there are signs of specific prejudices against women. Alan Wolfe cites a study in which a panel of male respondents was asked to rank the suitability of certain essays. When a man's name was listed as author, the evaluations tended to be higher; when a woman's name was given as author of the same essay, the terms "unscholarly" and "emotional" were more likely to be evoked. [11] This is hardly surprising since, even in childhood, young girls learn to devalue works written by women in men's fields. [12] Until recently, many productive women signed their articles with their first initials, rather than with their first, obviously feminine names. In many fields, they should not have abandoned this trick so quickly.

The third option—administration—is still virtually closed to women, even on campuses that draw their lower-echelon functionaries from faculty ranks. First, a woman will be unable to attract the attention of her colleagues, unless she learns the art of the end-run. An end-run occurs when a woman perceives that her immediate colleagues, perhaps feeling threatened by her, are unwilling to recognize her organizational and administrative ability. Abandoning her own departmental colleagues as hopeless, she turns to a faculty senate or the AAUP and establishes herself among men who are less directly threatened by her, being in completely different fields. Of course, she may not win at this gambit either, for the AAUP or senate may well contain a herd of intransigent chauvinists, and, at best, it will be years before her departmental colleagues are forced reluctantly to acknowledge her accomplishments elsewhere. Too, if she is untenured, she runs the risk of being fired as an overly aggressive AAUP president or union leader. But the gamble is well worth taking. Within the woman's own department, she will be given relatively few committee appointments. Of these, none will be important, unless it is possible to use her as a scapegoat, appointing her to chair a committee after its work has already been bungled beyond redemption.

Even on those rare occasions when a woman is given an honest appointment to a committee of some importance, her problems are not yet over. If she is new to the campus, she will promptly be put in her place—accidentally, of course. As she enters the meeting room for the first time, one of her colleagues rises to introduce her: "Dr. Gradgrind, this is Sally. Dr. Dryasdust, I want you to meet Sally. Sally is new here." Likely as not, if the woman is under six feet tall, the colleague affectionately ruffles Sally's hair. Naturally, it is assumed that Sally is a new secretary, there to take the minutes. For all anyone knows, she may have come to sweep the floor. What has been made obvious is that Sally has no status, and it would be considered vulgar self-advertisement for Sally to insist that she has the Ph.D. too. Thus Sally will be patronized. Her raised hand will be overlooked, and, should she insist on speaking, she will be heard with that benevolent tolerance with which parents listen to a mentally retarded child.

And, of course, she will be assigned to take the minutes, which effectively removes her from active participation in discussions anyhow. Which is just as well. Korda writes: "When a man criticizes, he is being constructive or obstructive, as the case may be; when a woman criticizes, she is being a bitch, or nagging, the worst of sins in the lexicon of male/female relationships." [13] Consequently, when a woman participates, she is faced with the alternatives of nodding and smiling through even the worst of male imbecilities or of allowing herself to be typed as a castrating shrew.

Given a choice, most women opt for the easy way, which turns out, in the long run, not to be easy at all. She smiles, is docile, and promises herself to keep her temper until she is tenured. Unfortunately, if possessed of any integrity, she will at some point be unable to hold her tongue, and sometimes she is not forgiven for it. (Laments Agnes de Mille: "Men give men second chances, never women, except as an act of courtship." [14]) As she begins to assert herself, she will evoke "the resentment men harbor against the women who disciplined them when they were boys." [15] It is highly unlikely that a woman will surmount all this to find herself in a prestigious administrative position. Some lack the tact, others the patience.

Professional difficulties in these early years are compounded by personal problems peculiar to the female. If the woman has postponed childbearing until completion of her degree, she will probably find herself nearing an age when she dare not put off pregnancy any longer. Yet, should she become pregnant, she will be typed as unprofessional, with the inevitable threat to her tenure. Moreover, the problem of proving competence will become entangled with the problems of child care, usually complicated further by a certain guilt at being a working mother (even when she privately suspects that she would be driven to batter the child if she were forced to be home with it all the time). Her guilt will be regularly reinforced by her colleagues: "I don't see why you can't stay home while the baby is young and needs her mother." To a great extent, the men are doing this because they themselves are threatened. If the woman professor can maintain her multiple roles with grace and style, then some well-educated faculty wives may consider going back to work too. Also this is a chance to impress other men by voicing the platitudes of machismo, so that even the woman's husband, fearing ridicule, may turn uncooperative, categorically refusing to change a diaper or to cart the offensive mess to the laundromat.

And sex hangs like a fog about any college campus, complicating the early years of both married and single women. Especially in smaller towns, where there is a dearth of female flesh unconnected with the college, no singles bars, and few opportunities to get together with female students in private, the arrival of a new woman professor is an occasion to be celebrated with tumescence. Unfortunately, the name of this game is changing. Often sexual overtures now tend to be public performances. Increasingly, they have little to do with sex itself and a great deal more to do with the lecher's appreciative audience of male colleagues. In other words, many sexual advances have frankly homosexual overtones. Korda offers another explanation: "These days, as men of a certain age find themselves forced to deal with a tougher and more realistic generation of women, a pass seems hardly worth making unless it's done in public, its real importance being the demonstration that one is still in there fighting. . . ." [16] Thus a full professor stumbles drunkenly across a crowded room to fumble with the clothing of a new assistant, shouting in her ear: "Hey, baby, does your bra feel empty?" Frantically, the woman tries to recall some soothing words from Amy Vanderbilt, while the men and their wives snicker—at her.

No woman can win at this game. Only at a few urban schools, even now, can a woman afford a "reputation." Her personal life will be used to attack her professional competence. So even if she wants an affair, which she probably does not, she would never dare. On the other hand, men have been known to avenge themselves for public put-downs, even when the men themselves have forced the confrontation in public. Complained one woman: "People keep thinking that women are flattered by male advances. And then the man thinks you're insulting him when you aren't, so he's apt to get even with you professionally. And men are often in a position to do it." In business offices, of course, the woman is often fired. In academe, personal vindictiveness of this kind may find its way into decisions concerning tenure and promotion. And, after the woman has experienced this sort of thing once, it will contaminate her relations with male colleagues thereafter. She never knows when another man will choose to make a pass, and, having done so, will retaliate, upset at her disinterest. She may become excessively wary. Her colleagues—for even the men who indulge themselves in such behavior are generally unconscious of what they are doing—accuse her of being paranoid, which naturally also works to her disadvantage when she is put up for promotion.

Because women rarely help other women, each one believes that she is the first woman ever to confront these problems. Until recently, there has been no place for her to go for advice and empathy. Only occasionally would a senior woman of strong nerves and great compassion offer her services. In the last few years, Female Mafia Families have gradually formed themselves on many larger campuses. Within the university, they serve as underground railways for female students who have suffered discrimination and who must be channeled to some new discipline or adviser, and they help women compare notes and compile information, the results of which often end in Health, Education, and Welfare or EEOC. But the banding of these women remains shrouded in mystery. Some women fear retaliation if they are known as feminists; others fear loss of status should they be known to associate with women from other disciplines, let alone students and secretaries.

This kind of banding has occurred because it meets a need. Normally, women have nowhere to go with their complaints. The departmental chairman will not be interested in a woman's child-care problems, and he will perceive her reports of sexual retaliation as a particularly vicious betrayal of his fellow males. Even professional problems, such as an oppressive teaching schedule, cannot usually be taken to the chairman. After all, it was probably the chairman who arranged the schedule. And, too, academic protocol is such that few problems can be taken directly to the source. Caplow and McGee write:

A professor will generally complain to his chairman only about matters which are beyond the latter's control, for to complain about a matter within the chairman's scope is to challenge his authority. Thus complaints about the chairman will be made to peers, one of whom will carry the tale to the chairman. In this way, the status of the peer is enhanced, since the act of making the complaint to him implies that he can do something about it. The peer, in turn, is able to confront the chairman because the complaint is not his own. As an intermediary, he is not challenging the chairman's authority and will not fear retaliation.[17]

Women are almost totally debarred from access to this system. The woman has no peers, as a rule, who will take her case to the chairman. Her peers are mostly male, and a large number of them will see no reason for her to complain, even if she is teaching twice the number of classes for half the pay. The few men who understand—the homosexuals, the misfits—are usually having too many problems of their own, and the chairman would be unlikely to listen to them anyway. The few extant female colleagues cannot usually afford to lose status by defending another woman. And they, too, would not be given a hearing if they did.

Even on those few campuses with established grievance procedures, the same problems remain to haunt women. Grievance panels are usually selected from the tenured faculty. Since most faculty members are male, the chances are that an all-male panel will be called; because panel members must be tenured, it is hardly likely that the panel will include sympathetic young male radicals. On a small campus, some of the panel members will doubtless be friends of the woman's chairman and will share his attitudes. Moreover, many tenured faculty members deny the right of the untenured to protest *any* decisions made by senior staff. Even in cases where procedural standards and even freedom of speech have been flagrantly violated, panel members may still insist that the grievant is unjustified in appealing a negative tenure decision. They tend to be even more hostile to complaints by women and blacks who, many feel, are already unfairly protected.

There are other factors too in cases involving women. Sitting in deliberations, a panel member may laugh off the complaint altogether: "Oh, I know old Al who is chairman over there, and he's a good man. He tells me that woman is nothing but a neurotic." Or: "Yeah, they shouldn't have given her all that work if they were only going to pay her for half time, but, look, have you ever found a way to keep a dumb broad from making a fool of herself. Hell, she walked into that, and it's her own fault." Or: "You know, that woman broke down and cried—I couldn't believe it —when we heard her case. And she's trying to tell us she's competent and shouldn't be fired—would you believe it?" Sometimes, mixed in with such comments, there is a perceptible degree of sadistic glee. For a few of these men, this is the first time they have had extensive power over a woman's life, and they are enjoying every minute of it. Others simply assume that women are supposed to suffer, and Professor Smith cannot be a very good woman if she is going to complain about her lot. And, of late, greed enters in. To raise a woman's salary is to take money away from a man—or so some men believe. Where financial exigency exists and enrollments are dropping, faculty members fear mass firings. To them, every woman who is retained jeopardizes a job held by a man. Fair and impartial treatment, while it sometimes occurs, is hardly to be expected under the circumstances.

It would seem that paranoia is the only sensible reaction to the state of affairs, but the fact of the matter is that flexible and moderately well-balanced female personalities adjust remarkably well sooner or later. It is possible to make friends by looking for individuals, within and without one's own discipline, so long as one is not concerned with status. The woman can always argue truthfully that she could never really have been part of the status system anyhow. What is more, if the woman has not totally lost her emotional balance and sense of humor, it is possible to find friends among the men, provided one does not expect too much. It is possible to laugh at the social climbers, at the constipated old boys network, and at oneself, for having foolishly wandered into it. Professionally there are end-runs, and, in the absence of library facilities and time, academic journalism can be substituted for academic research with the result that (1) the woman will have published enough to qualify for a better job, and (2) she will find herself—eventually—esteemed by her colleagues, most of whom will not bother to read her articles and could not tell the difference between journalism and scholarship if they did.

The problem is that all academic personalities are not well balanced, flexible, self-sacrificing, and good humored. As we have seen, many of the women who will end up with academic appointments have been programmed from the cradle for disaster. And, as we have also seen, the academic community offers an almost ideal set of catalysts to ensure that these disasters will be precipitated.

Circe is the most predictable of the lot. She may have dressed in a tailored suit for her interview, but, from her first day on the job, she will arrive at work clad like a streetwalker. With ungoverned breasts bobbing gently and expanses of thigh and rump exposed on every staircase, she gazes tenderly into the eyes of her new colleagues, who obligingly hyperventilate. Entering their offices, she is not content to sit in a chair. Instead, she walks around the desk to lean over the man's shoulder. If a breast brushes against his ear as she points to a line on a page, it can hardly be blamed on her. After all, her style of dress and her behavior are "natural," and it is not her fault that all men are nasty-minded beasts.

Were she to consider herself a permanent employee, she might be shocked into changing her behavior, but she has not yet considered that she may be forced to work with these men for twenty or thirty years. She considers her new job an extension of graduate—and high and elementary—school. It is a place for her to loiter and to flirt. In a few years, she will find something new to do and she will go away or maybe she will even grit her teeth and settle down to marry. She has virtually no notion that tenure guidelines might cause someone else to make certain decisions for her and to send her off before she is ready.

Thus her defenses are designed only for this transient state. She protects herself from men by being elusive. Consciously or not, she flirts only in broad daylight, with the office door open. She bats her eyelashes by the mailbox; she coos in the hallways; she lounges seductively at department meetings. When she attends parties, she is accompanied by another woman or by an amiable married couple: "But Professor Chowderhead and his wife were so kind to bring me . . . I just couldn't go off with someone else." Nonetheless, in a year or two, she will have had some kind of sexual confrontation with half the men on the staff, and she will have insulted all of them in the attempt to avoid the consequences of her own actions. And, incidentally, she will have made life more difficult for the many other women who do not welcome their colleagues' advances, for the men find it convenient to believe that all academic women would be as provocative as Circe, if only they knew how.

Circe's last line of defense, however, is especially infuriating to most men. Cornered, she turns on the man, complaining bitterly and frequently of being treated as a sex object. Even if she is not a feminist, she can fall back on general moral outrage, for, as is obvious, she is now a fullfledged participant in the nasty little game that Eric Berne christened "Rapo" in the second degree (also called "Indignation"). In this game, the female participant "gets only secondary satisfaction" from the male's advances, being primarily gratified by the opportunity of rejecting him.[18] After all, both traditional writings and the essays of recent feminists reassure her that all men are vicious and pretty well deserve what happens to them. What is more, Circe may well insist, sexual behavior of any sort is permissible, so long as the woman retains her technical chastity, a concept that will not be outmoded until it can no longer be used as an excuse for ugly games.

For about six months, then, Circe will be the most popular employee in the place. She is a delight to have around —for awhile. She is not threatening. With her, no man is forced to *prove* his virility, and it will take about six months of the dinners and cocktail parties to which she is not invited before every man realizes that he is most decidedly not the only man in her life. In the interim, Circe provides all the delights of the bordello without its sexual threats and all the fantasies of the ideal romance without the responsibilities of car payments and diaper services, and each of her co-workers can imagine that she cares for him alone. Circe, of course, is only half-conscious of what she is doing and of the reactions she is provoking. Her habits are well formed by now, and she has little cause to think about them. She is only somewhat perplexed by the attention so many men seem to pay her.

Unfortunately, Circe does not take advantage of this period of grace to establish herself professionally. Probably she could hardly tolerate libraries and laboratories for long enough to complete her dissertation; the ego reinforcement she needs is not to be found among test tubes and dusty books. She will have emerged from graduate school in a state of active rebellion against the cloistered life there, and she is now happy to allow her social relationships to consume her precious time. In other words, she runs into all the normal obstacles to publication, plus a few new ones she has invented for herself. With any luck, she may manage a few book reviews, a few brief notes. But she will have trouble even with these, since men will not take her seriously enough to help her place them, and the older women despise her. Of late, she may well settle for publishing an article on consciousness-raising or on the generally malevolent nature of males, only to find later that this will not count for much when a committee of men decides on her tenure.

In the classroom, she evokes hostility. Student evaluations are likely to show that, in her long and obvious flirtations with male students and colleagues, she has won little respect from anybody. A few male students will have succumbed to adolescent crushes, which is something else that happens whenever new female professors weigh less than 250 pounds and are more prepossessing than the Gorgon. These students, being vulnerable, she will put down with greater ferocity than she would dare use toward her colleagues. Most male adolescents have sexual problems enough without all this. They turn on her vengefully, even if they cannot always articulate the reasons for their anger. A few radical student feminists may recognize the castrating wrath behind her feminine exterior and may form a clique to support her, but they will not be effective defenders against her male judges. More conventional women students quietly detest her, for she seems to be competing with them for the attention of every available male, however young.

Medea, on the other hand, has a sixth sense for the academic power structure, and it takes her no time at all to realize that women are not a part of it. Predictably, then, she will pretend to be a man, and she will demand to be treated as such (although privately she still may be insulted when men regard her as unfeminine). What actually happens is that she sets herself up as the probable victim of guerrilla warfare. At first, her male colleagues admire her feistiness; little by little, as they realize she is serious in her demands for recognition, their admiration turns into ridicule. In essence, Dr. Frankenstein is taking another long look at his fabrication and is learning that, on a day-to-day basis, such a creature makes an utterly intolerable companion. Of course, Medea is blamed, although having learned one set of reactions she has no choice but to repeat them interminably. When she finds that only men are given free time for research, she throws a fit; when she learns that she is expected to teach freshman history sections, she harangues; when she is given an exceptionally heavy teaching schedule, she orates. And, when she learns that polished shoes and a fashionable wife are more important than professional publications, she shrieks. Inevitably, she wins at least one victory, and, clinging to that one laurel, she will see no reason to change her ways. Instead, her scenes, set speeches, and occasional almost hysterical frenzy will increase in frequency and intensity as her problems escalate, and she will be, without question, a certifiable nuisance.

Nonetheless, she protects herself very well. Since she works best in solitude and since solitude is the natural condition for new female assistant professors, she will probably be unusually productive, and, despite all obstacles, she may quickly and adeptly establish a substantial publication list. After all, blank pages do not talk back to her, and most communications with editors and publishers are (1) written and (2) infrequent. She may find herself embroiled in exceptionally numerous and bitter scholarly controversies, but she will attribute their singularly nasty tone to the paranoiac jealousy of Vested Interests or to the influence of Envious Colleagues at her own school—aware that no one likes her much, she likes to think that this is the result of Conspiracies Formed Against Her. True, in a few years, certain editors will blanch and flee upon hearing her name in convention corridors. But until recently there has been no scarcity of markets for most scholarly writing, and even now there are new journals emerging in Holland and Japan. Medea will exploit all of them. She has decided that publication is her forte. Her salary is spent flying to distant libraries or research centers on weekends, and her husband—if she has one—is put on a diet of TV dinners.

But writing today is seldom enough, and Medea's teaching career will be punctuated by student protest. It is remotely possible, of course, that she will be applauded as a superb classroom lecturer. Students enjoy verbal pyrotechnics, and this is Medea's field of expertise. Nevertheless, practically every other aspect of teaching depends upon human communication, and communication presupposes participation by more than one party, a concept that increasingly disconcerts Medea. After a few years in her classroom and her study, she will have forgotten that other people have a right to talk too.

Consequently, her chairman will spend an irritating amount of time with her students. She will have raged at one because the student questioned her views, and she will storm at another because he sought to change a grade. She will have had a full-fledged tantrum when a student —cavalier, as are most students today, as to catalogue requirements—failed to take Afghanistan History 101 as prerequisite for her own course in Siberian Culture. Everyone but Medea will have forgotten that the former was ever on the books or that it was a prerequisite for anything. In his idle moments, her chairman will try to calm her as, appalled by the failure of the university to live up to her standards, she storms in to demand that he instantaneously reform student manners and morals, insist on merit as a basis for peer judgment, reinstate a proper seriousness toward academic protocol, and reverse current economic trends, so that it is not necessary for colleges to accept just any student. *She* has standards. She is incapable of admitting (1) that anyone could legitimately have different ones, (2) that it is impossible to keep some academic men from having none at all, and (3) that the *Zeitgeist* can exert certain pressures of its own.

She will be appointed to committees, if only because of the force of her intransigent will, and, realizing that her publication record is sounder than that of her colleagues, she will perceive such appointments as an invitation to take over the world—the first step toward higher administration. Unfortunately, she is insulted by the existence of Robert's Rules of Order. Possessed of fierce pride and, sometimes, fierce integrity, she is rude and abrasive in her refusal to be squelched, as Circe and so many others are squelched, and it never even occurs to her to exercise the option of keeping quiet, as so many other women and men learn to do. Moreover, she takes all this very seriously and thus becomes a figure of ridicule. Men know that, with rare exceptions, academic committees have more to do with Parkinson's Law than anything else and mainly provide an opportunity for males to size up each others' verbal and manipulative skills. Tragically, Medea's ideals are less ignoble than theirs, and, on academic issues, she is often dead right. But it is her neurotic self-assertiveness that will be remembered, not her views. After a while, few committee appointments any longer come her way and she begins to suspect another Plot.

Medusa is quickly reduced to a negligible role. Bedraggled creature that she is, she is handed four or five classes of remedial something-or-other, and, for her reward, she is given an occasional term on the Spring Retirement Banquet committee—if anyone happens to remember her existence. Nor can she get started as a researcher. Because she has always been someone's self-effacing assistant, she is incapable of propelling herself into action, and she may be too insecure to express herself unabetted in print. She needs the sanction and protection of some male superior, but her superiors will not now give this reinforcement. She would want articles signed under her own name, not theirs. Where she was once cheap scab labor, she is now a threat, a potential competitor in the race for scarce research funds. Her graduate professors once soothed and reassured her, if only out of pity, when she asked for information and advice. Now the same kind of request elicits a snarl. "I shouldn't have to waste my time with your problems," she is told. Being Medusa, she is convinced that she is once more in the wrong, a conviction that does nothing to raise her self-esteem. Morosely, she goes home and throws another article into the incinerator, not the mailbox.

Consequently, she is dependent upon her reputation as a classroom teacher. And inevitably in the teaching situation the male students automatically reflect their elders' pity and contempt. They see how she is regarded by her male colleagues. What is more, they have been trained from birth to believe that a homely or dowdy woman has nothing to offer. Female students, of course, recoil from her in horror, for she reminds them of the grimmest spinster teachers of their earlier years, and they fear to be identified with such losers. Nor will she have support from feminists, who are not usually interested in her kinds of problems. Evaluations of her teaching, when solicited, will reflect these emotional reactions. They may have little to do with her actual teaching proficiency, but no tenure or promotion committee will take this into account.

On the other hand, unless they are vociferous radicals, Penelope and Hebe are merely cloaked in invisibility. Both are touchingly grateful for their jobs, and they are tempted to express their gratitude in the only ways they know. Hebe tries to seduce the chairman. Penelope makes coffee every morning and brings cookies from home. Neither woman has any strong sense of professionalism; neither possesses what Beauvoir regards as a transcendental mentality. Nor have they seriously considered problems of tenure, salary, promotion, or even personal accomplishment. Raising of salary and granting of tenure, they assume, are routine. In fact, Hebe is not even around much, so she does not hear the problems that others are having, while Penelope assumes, in some twisty way, that being a good woman is enough. When Hebe is supposed to be keeping office hours, she is in the student union with a tormented drug freak, just as Penelope tends to wander from her office to discuss her family or children or glands with the secretaries. During the first few years, the men do not bother to learn their names, unless there is some reason for them to be patronized or mocked at faculty cocktail parties.

For both, sexual functions will tend to dominate their lives, for they take their salaries for granted. Chances are good that Hebe will become pregnant and will want to keep the illegitimate child. Under current laws, she will probably finagle maternity leave, and she will blithely ignore her male colleagues' shock. She will assume that they cannot fire her for this, which is true. What they can fire her for—and she seldom understands this—is her professional irresponsibility as she ignores faculty meetings, drones tediously through her lecture notes, and laughs at any notion of duties outside class contact hours. Penelope, on the other hand, seems incompetent because she is playing Perfect Female Employee. She meets her classes; she does what she is told—nothing more and nothing less. She assumes that men will give her sound advice; sometimes she assumes this even when she is a feminist and should know better. If they tell her she must forfeit her tenure to take maternity leave, she forfeits her tenure. Only later, when money grows scarce and she is dismissed from her job, does she come vaguely to suspect that the men were not looking out for her best interests after all.

Of these women, though, Hebe and Penelope are likely to be allowed to drag their weary weights along for many years, barring any real budget crisis—when they will be fired. After all, they have been hired cheaply; they are useful for staffing undesirable sections. Apparently, too, they never complain. Some departmental legalist may point out that these women will come up for tenure, promotion, and salary raises, just as if they were human, but administrators of all ranks are eager to shrug this fact off. Cheap female labor has been used for decades, and they find it difficult to believe that women will not be content with this, their natural lot. The new militancy of the 1960's and 1970's, they assume, is merely a passing fad, as is Affirmative Action. After all, the last woman they fired—1967, was it?—went quietly, and it is to be assumed that all decent women will do the same.

7

From Female Grievance
to Feminist Insurrection

Contrary to popular academic opinion, female grievances do not vanish when ignored. Instead they tend to metamorphosize into full-scale law suits and into appeals to a variety of state and federal agencies. Too often, administrators and male faculty assume that such appeals are provoked by a small body of radical feminists and that feminism itself is a (200-year-old) fad. Both assumptions are erroneous. Moreover, the pursuit of equity is grounded in many other significant phenomena of our time. It has something to do with the new consumerism—many women professors are paying taxes to support the very institutions that overwork and underpay them. It has something to do with white-collar collective bargaining, as well as with a variety of other societal changes. And it has a great deal to do with younger academics' disillusionment with the Colonel Blimpism that too often masquerades as academic excellence, with the failure of the establishment to tolerate independent thought, and with the cynical insistence of graduate professors on producing new doctoral candidates for whom no jobs could possibly exist. Only recently, however, have women found an effective way of evidencing their own loss of faith. As Georgina M. Smith writes: "Until 1970, the woman professor who knew she was being short-changed could expect nothing but sympathy from the federal and state agencies and the courts." [1] Although too often with glacial slowness, that situation began to change when Dr. Bernice Sandler, working through the Women's Equity Action League, filed a class complaint of sex discrimination against all public and private colleges and universities holding federal contracts.

Since then, there has been a flood of such complaints. Despite their apparent prolixity and complexity, however, grievances can mostly be lumped into three classifications. First, there are those involving termination of employment or denial of tenure which can, ostensibly, be played out under the Queensberry Rules laid down in the AAUP handbook—if the institution is willing to play by any rules at all, which some are not. In many tenure cases, faculty and administration are acting in good faith; denial of tenure is a genuine attempt to rid the institution of an incompetent. It is reasonable, for example, to expect teachers to meet with their classes, and it is equally reasonable to expect the teacher to evidence some passing interest or knowledge in the field for which he was hired. Certainly, the timid female spirit who breaks into tears when confronted by a room full of even the most docile students should be encouraged to pursue another line of work, as should the black cross-country coach who, in a fit of absent-mindedness, precipitates his team over the edge of a cliff. Mixed with these will be a few quasi-legitimate denials, in which the minority employee has been naïve enough to walk into an ambush arranged by chauvinist hustlers among her immediate peers. When no administrator has taken well-publicized steps to halt this second kind of dismissal, there will be an occasional epidemic of these cases. As a result, the entire retention policy of the college may be called into question and this will lead in turn to legal suits and to the unwelcome public airing of academic dirty linen.

In recent years, of course, a second class of problems has emerged, caused by fiscal exigency—or alleged exigency. Roughly translated, this means that the promoters are refusing to put up the money, the heat and lights have been shut off, and now some of the players must be conned into going away. Here again certain institutions have legitimate problems, although the plea of exigency should usually be viewed with the gravest suspicion. When a college is willing to open its books to public or legal scrutiny, the problem is apt to be genuine. On the other hand, some administrators simply announce: "There's exigency when I say there's exigency." And that is another matter entirely. Often, as the budget tightens, a laissez-faire policy develops as a function of administrative laziness, ineptitude, or fear of losing the support of a predominantly male faculty. Rather than examining the entire budget and personnel policy (which might result in the dismissal of several superfluous administrators and a half-dozen long-hopeless faculty drunks), the administration turns its collective head as the faculty concentrates on scuttling the most

vulnerable of its members. Automatically, that means females, especially since male faculty members are almost
totally ignorant of recent legal precedents.

A third type of problem appears when women, reading
of what has been happening elsewhere, suddenly decide
that they have long been underpaid. Or that a dispropor-
tionate number of women remain permanently at the lower
ranks, while equally incompetent males are promoted. Or
a woman on half-time appointment begins to wonder why
she is working as many hours as the men for only half the
pay. Maternity-leave problems fall into this miscellaneous
assortment. So do the problems of black and chicano to-
kens, many of them women. Hired in the first frenzy of
Affirmative Action, they discover years later that they are
neither full-time faculty nor full-time administrators. Their
jobs were invented for the occasion, and they are protected neither by tenure nor by anything else. There are
no guidelines for handling most of these problems, although some may be funneled to a faculty grievance committee (and the problems inherent in this have already
been suggested). Usually, there is a refusal to admit that
these are problems at all, the rationale—apparently—being that any problem that did not exist in 1880 has no real
academic standing. Even among the best-intentioned, the
tendency is to form a committee to study the matter, and
the committee deliberations tend to go on year after year,
as the women look on helplessly.

Naturally, female protestations grow more vehement,
finally attracting the attention of male faculty members
who are collectively surprised, appalled, and uncooperative. By this time, the women believe that they are faced
with intransigent ill-will (actually, they are faced with

what the Roman Catholic Church has termed invincible ignorance), and this leads to the third and least manageable stage of protest. At this point, abandoning what rules there are, the women take to the streets. Caucuses will be formed. Administrative offices will be besieged by grievants. The women will have consulted lawyers and will have called in several state and federal mediators, while the problems themselves will grow fuzzy around the edges and will include complaints that are not altogether legitimate. By now the activity will attract the attention of higher administration, whose turn it is to be surprised and appalled. But administrators and faculty will seize upon the least legitimate of the women's grievances, using certain of the less rational complaints as an excuse for taking none of the problems seriously. So the women file with the government. Most of the time, all of this happens in a more or less predictable sequence which, with a minimal amount of administrative vigilance and faculty integrity, could be interrupted at any point.

Obviously, there are two kinds of campus where this will not be true. At one extreme, there is the small private or religious college that has never attempted to establish any approximation of due process. Administration and a few powerful faculty govern, indulging themselves in fine, Renaissance excesses of decision-making, and the female victim has no way to discern the difference between sexual discrimination and the free-floating whimsicality by which the school is normally administered. While many of these schools hold federal contracts and can be forced into compliance with government regulations, the sensible woman will avoid the schools altogether, even at the risk of being forced into another line of work. She might better benefit, for example, by learning bordello management, for her profits will be higher, her employment more secure, her tasks perhaps less degrading, and her hours certainly shorter. At the more haphazard of colleges, she will be subject to every chauvinistic flight of fantasy, she will be expected to grovel in appreciation of a probably wretched teaching schedule, she will be unable to make any case on the basis of violation of due process, there being no process, and her miserable wages will not even afford her a competent attorney. At the opposite extreme is the megaversity where, for quite different reasons, women are also alienated, even from contact with other women. Due to geographical or urban sprawl, faculty is scattered. So many women are employed that some are certain to be equitably treated, and the ones who are not do not know about each other. Usually communication is so poor that faculty members are not even aware of internal grievance procedures, if any exist. Some faculty women will never even have encountered an administrator on the hoof. Naturally, the aggrieved woman here will go directly to HEW or to some similar bureau. She has no way of knowing what else to do.

Most campuses fall somewhere between these extremes. Some effort will have been made to define policy, and lip-service will have been paid to Affirmative Action guidelines. Some campus women will have been involved in the faculty senate, the AAUP, a collective bargaining group, or in departmental decision-making, and many of these will at first try to pursue equity through established channels, if any. Only when administrators and male faculty repeatedly ignore obviously symptomatic individual grievances will the situation threaten to escalate completely out of hand.

1. The First Step: The Traditional Guidelines That Do Not Quite Work

On many campuses, female disenchantment first seems to express itself as a result of some questionable tenure decision, for, as Betty Chmaj writes, "the resistance to awarding tenure to women is particularly great and seems particularly unjustified." [2] A decade ago, the woman who was denied tenure would have quietly skulked away. Now, more cognizant of her rights and of the pitfalls built into the system, she protests and frequently publicizes her case, at least informally. This, in turn, serves as a focal point. Younger, untenured women see what may happen to them when they come up against the system. The resultant squabble may even alert older women to problems (including their own salaries) that they had previously preferred to ignore. In other words, the publicizing of one breakdown in the system calls attention to all the others.

And the tenure system is susceptible to breaking down because the probationary period, as a rule, is ill defined. Most modestly efficient universities have statutes which spell out the length of the probationary period, usually ranging from one or two years to the seven-year maximum authorized by the AAUP. Unfortunately, that is all the statutes—or anything else—spell out, although practically any time period would do, provided standards for achieving tenure were clearly stated to the candidate, who

should also be made aware of any evaluation of his performance and given opportunity to remedy its deficiencies.
J. Douglas Brown who, as emeritus provost and dean of
faculty at Princeton, could hardly be considered a flaming
young radical, long ago urged the need for regular review.
Under his plan, there would be a five-year probationary
period. The annual reviews would be followed by serious
evaluation at the end of the third year. After this, only
those candidates would be retained who were deemed
eligible for promotion; the rest would be dismissed at the
end of a one-year terminal contract.[3] Such a system would
be as fair as any, provided the candidate were fully informed and involved at every step in the proceedings.

The reason why such systems only rarely exist, however,
becomes transcendently clear at this point: no one has the
faintest idea as to how a candidate should be evaluated.
If the candidate presses the issue, he will be given a faculty
handbook, which will do him little good, especially as his
chairman has not read it. At worst, this handbook insists
that the candidate be a good man and true, a phrase cleverly calculated to make female candidates a bit skittish.
At best, the handbook vaguely alludes to combinations of
publication, service, and excellence in teaching. The candidate then realizes that what she really needs to know
is how to read the minds, if any, of her colleagues. About
this time, as she slowly recognizes the absence of objective standards, the untenured woman becomes embittered,
if not enraged, at the faculty social events to which she
was not invited, the faculty club stag parties which she
could not attend, and the all-pervasive influence of faculty
wives.

Nonetheless, her career is in the hands of her immediate

colleagues, although even faculty members sometimes express doubt as to the singular fitness of faculty to make these decisions out of hand. In a survey of professors at a Midwest university, Archie R. Dykes found that fewer than half of the 106 respondents favored total faculty autonomy in these matters. Their skepticism, he writes, apparently derives from "a belief that faculty members tend to permit friendships and personal biases to influence their decisions unduly." One respondent referred to a professorial tendency "to become soft in the head." [4] Although unaware of Dykes's findings, the female candidate may have begun thinking along the same line.

Since individual cases develop eccentrically from this point, let us take as an example the case of Circe Veneering, the brunette bombshell. Circe, hired into the English department of a small state school, has generally given a dismal performance. Enmeshed in her private woes, she teaches listlessly from her graduate school notes. Unfortunately, she attended a third-rate graduate school and took poor notes, and it is obvious that the students are avoiding her classes. Too, Circe has not published. At meetings, she has heard the senior staff complain that they themselves cannot publish without research funds and released time. Since she has been given neither, she has assumed that publication would not be required of her. Had her chairman noticed she was still on the staff, he might have terminated her contract years before, but the one time he thought of doing so, he realized that he could not hire anyone else for as little money. So he forgot about her until just recently. Under normal conditions, denying her tenure would be a matter of routine.

As the date for the tenure decision approaches, Circe

grows uneasy and visits her chairman. Crossing her legs, pulling up her skirt, and thrusting out her bosom, she asks about her situation. Her chairman is obviously aghast. Circe assumes he is intimidated by her physical presence. Actually, he is appalled by her violation of academic protocol. She should not be directly questioning him; she should have known how to read the subtle signals he gave her. Academics, as Jessie Bernard has pointed out, are "notoriously sensitive" to slights, brooding over the most minuscule bits of evidence that "they are not valued as highly as a colleague." [5] During the past months, knowing that Circe was coming up for tenure, he has deliberately slighted her and has encouraged his cronies to follow suit. Circe has been excluded from certain social events, has not been given released time for research, has been appointed to no committees. What he has forgotten is that no woman in his department has been invited to these social functions, none has been given released time, and none has been appointed to committees. The traditional signal system cannot work. First, Circe could know about these signals only if she were invited to the in-group social gatherings where the put-downs are discussed. Second, because most women are treated shoddily, Circe would have no particular reason to take the signals personally, even if she knew what they were. On the other hand, her chairman, irritated by what he considers her outrageously unprofessional performance, could not explain the need for such a signal system if he tried. The status quo has no rationale, nor, he thinks, should it.

A week later, Circe is back, having received a negative decision. "What does this mean?" she demands, none too politely. She is not used to being foiled by males. "Well, er—," says the chairman, puffing his pipe (or cigar, or cigarette, for smoking, as any student knows, is the academic way of avoiding direct declarative statements, which is why it is so hard to curb smoking in the classroom). "We've denied you tenure," he finally says, brightly.

But Circe knows that quite a different decision was handed down on Mr. Tallboy, who plays golf with the chairman at the faculty club and sings in his choir on Sunday. She asks about Mr. Tallboy. Her chairman insists that Tallboy is the better teacher. Pressed, he admits he cannot prove it, no form of evaluation being used in either case. But he is sure of it, just the same. Neither has published. Mr. Tallboy, however, has served on a number of committees.

"But you yourself appointed him to all those committees," she whimpers. "How can you penalize me for not serving when you never appointed me. You haven't let me do anything at all." "You didn't seem interested," says the chairman, and terminates the interview with the remark: "After all, Mr. Tallboy has a family to support."

With anguish in her heart, Circe watches the chairman march off to lunch—with her dean and Mr. Tallboy. Later she pursues the matter with the dean, only to encounter another variation of the Chauvinist Gavotte. Women being a nuisance, the dean passes the matter on to a higher dean or provost, who slyly passes the responsibility upward to the board of trustees. The board, being made up of some combination of conservative bankers, farmers, preachers, or priests, gives Circe's case short shrift, which is what everyone, except perhaps Circe, knew would happen. Then Circe's dean tenderly and sympathetically explains: "I tried, but what can you expect of bankers,

farmers, preachers, or priests?" Meanwhile, Circe is co-
cooned among sympathetic women, most of whom loathe
Mr. Tallboy, who is something of a hustler. They urge
Circe to take her case to the government. What matters
if Circe is incompetent, so long as the department persists
in rewarding equal incompetence among the males?

Across campus, several other women are suffering similar experiences. There is, for example, Medusa, who is the
foreordained victim of a set-up. In this case, the bête noir
is Professor Borgia. Hired the same year as Medusa, he has
evidenced an all-encompassing sympathy with her many
social and professional failures. In her gratitude, she
spends her time proofreading his articles when she should
be writing her own, but then he has assured her that publication is not really worth worrying about. When he com-
pliments her on a new dress, she gratefully volunteers to
write a lengthy library report to which Professor Borgia
signs his name. On the basis of that report, Professor
Borgia is appointed undergraduate adviser, a position
which allows him solicitously to offer his help in evalu-
ating teaching—including the teaching of those who will
compete with him for tenure and promotion. "They'd be
more comfortable with me," he assures his chairman, "than
with some senior professor they hardly know." A charm-
ing chap, he is allowed carte blanche by his chairman,
who does not want to be bothered with such matters anyway. And Borgia already knows who is popular. He knows
who has been invited to the right parties, who has curried
favor with the college president. These people receive excellent marks, since Borgia knows he could not hurt them
if he tried. Medusa is a different matter. After observing
her classes, he returns to his chairman, on his face an ex-

pression of great sadness: "Don't make me write the report. I just can't do that to a friend." The chairman is touched by his sensitivity. Medusa, informed that she has been denied tenure because she has not published and because Borgia found her teaching to be inadequate, is likewise moved, if not precisely in the same way. Even Medusa's brand of self-flagellation has its limits.

It is unlikely that either case will be reversed. However, since the job market has toughened and tenure denials consequently become more frequent, those denied, less aware of a stigma, are now willing to admit and compare their experiences. And, as a result of the new feminism, women are more willing to talk with each other. Medusa and Circe are now going to see their terminations as a function of discrimination, not as a result of their own inadequacies, although in their cases the truth lies somewhere between. But both, before they seek other jobs, alert the surviving women on campus to the possibilities of discrimination: the women become suspicious, suddenly recalling like instances in the past. Circe has hired a lawyer and takes Medusa to see him, and the lawyer, hearing their gossip, begins to envision himself as the first Affirmative Action attorney in the area. Reading up on court cases, he dreams of suits for back pay; he contemplates an early retirement to Capri.

2. Fiscal Exigency, More or Less

Rumors circulate around the campus. Money is tight. Chairmen whisper of the need to terminate faculty. In some departments, new young scholars are looking for ways to rid themselves of the senior citizens; elsewhere the old guard has designs upon the salaries of the young turks. Where there are women, though, the department speaks as with a single voice: "Scuttle them first." Naturally, some of the women are married. These women— or so the men assume—have no right to work. Of course, many of their own wives are employed, but that is different; they need the extra money to get the kids through college. Married women faculty have no excuse. They just want to be contrary, to take bread from the mouths of the men's starving families. Some of the other women are single. Obviously, if these women were not working, they would find husbands, settle down, and be much happier. It would almost be doing them a favor to fire them.

At this point, intervention by a strong administrative figure is essential. As Robert P. Quinn (*et al.*) found in a study of industrial anti-Semitism, "the ancient principle of *noblesse oblige* should weigh most heavily on top managers. If they will not honor a policy of promotion according to ability, who can be expected to do so?" [6] Just as, in industry, top management is most aware of specific personnel policies, so in academic administration, top management is most cognizant of the law. Thus, as the Quinn study shows, administration is responsible for making it clear that policy, not personal attitudes, will dictate decision-making, and top administrators must also take time to identify those who are personally disposed to deviate from policy and to review their decisions. [7] Such examination naturally takes time, but the strategic administrative appointment of a woman to a high post would serve as an adequate example in the interim.

Usually, neither the appointment nor the examination

occurs. Of course, thanks to black activism in the past, the college may well have an Affirmative Action policy, but in practice the effect of that policy is sabotaged. The mere knowledge that there is no woman in higher administration is evidence enough that the policy regarding women will not be taken seriously. Also the same administrators who pay lip-service to Affirmative Action in the office wink and reiterate the same old chauvinistic obscenities at cocktail parties and three-martini lunches. And, as the Quinn study shows, "Top management's influence is far more potent in its *example* than in its *directives*." [8] Perceiving administrative inaction for what it is, chairmen and faculty continue to write off Affirmative Action for women as a passing fad.

Unless terminations are directed by a college president or board, tenured women will not be among the first to be dismissed. Too many faculty men are jealous of tenure, sensibly realizing that they themselves could be placed in jeopardy should they allow any encroachments on the system. What happens, then, is the sacrifice of the lambs, many of whom have been bleating their way toward the abattoir for years. More than likely, for example, the first step will be a proposal for a tenure quota or even a moratorium on tenure. While apparently innocuous, a quota or moratorium serves effectively to protect the status quo. The highest percentage of women and of minority persons, in most cases, will have been hired in the past several years as a direct result of government pressures. These people are only beginning to come up for tenure. Now, where quotas or moratoria are put into effect, their chairman can tell them, sympathetically, that while he himself would like to grant tenure, his hands are tied because of the action of the university. Thus the woman, the chicano, the black are forced to wander from school to school. For many years they may swell a college's Affirmative Action statistics without ever being allowed to become full-fledged members of any staff.

Somewhere too, for example, there will be women who have allowed themselves to be professionally fragmented. Take Penelope Wombly, a wife and mother who has been touchingly grateful for any employment at all. In her grati-tude, she has allowed a third of her time to be filled in counselling, a third in teaching sex and marriage, and a third in teaching the xylophone. The three-thirds, she thinks, total up to a full-time job. Actually, they do not, for few departments assume responsibility for continued employment or tenure of anyone who has less than a half-time assignment with that department. Only the people who do the hiring, however, know this and they have never found it necessary to explain the situation to the people—mostly women—who are hired in this manner. Penelope has never given the matter any thought. After all, she has been employed for more than 20 years, and surely the school has some responsibility. (It has none.) When money tightens, sex and xylophones are suddenly seen as the frivolities that have to go, and so does Pene-lope. She seeks other jobs, only to be told that she is too old; the years have slipped by, her hair has turned white, and she has nothing in the way of genuinely professional credentials behind her. Tearfully, she comes back to con-sult with the AAUP or the union and with other women on campus. No one can or will help her. Penelope has al-lowed herself to be exploited, and that is the end of it. But the female survivors, already upset by suspicious tenure denials, now are deeply disturbed. They snoop around. What they find is that the few men hired in such lunatic fashion have been transferred to full-time employment in one of the departments; it was only the women who were fired. Now Penelope will write the government.

Penelope's case is followed in short order by that of Hebe, who for 15 years has alternated between "part-time" and "temporary" employment. Lora H. Robinson, in a survey of "temporary" faculty women at Michigan State University, found that of 153 "temporary" women, 13 had been employed for 10 years or more, two assistant professors for 24 years, and one instructor for 25 years.[9] Hebe, who alternates between teaching the fluegelhorn, ceramics, and freshman English as the need arises, has never been much concerned with her professional status. She is not even quite sure how she got her job in the first place, for she was hired by that process which has been somewhat bitterly described by D. B. Gowin and George H. Daigneault:

. . . when student enrollment bulges, a dean . . . picks up the telephone and calls for a part-time instructor. The instructor is selected by these criteria: can he teach at a specified time . . . for a small amount of money? He is "prepared" for teaching by a talk with the dean, by an introduction to a full-time faculty person, by an invitation to the one dinner held during the semester, and by a handbook which may or may not be given him. He is told where the class meets, where his mail box is, and when he will receive his check . . .[10]

Mostly, Hebe is interested in the money, which allows her to support herself minimally while (1) caring for her children or (2) finding lovers or (3) mimeographing for some radical cause. As often happens, though, Hebe is a good teacher, and intellectual curiosity has led her to complete the Ph.D. over a period of years, until she is as well qualified as the regular members of a somewhat lethargic staff. Also she has come to think of herself as a fixture. When she is terminated, she is shocked; she is told that the school is terminating all part-time employees, it being only coincidental that almost all are women. Naturally, Hebe asks if she could be given a full-time appointment. She is told that her colleagues do not consider her competent enough for that. Naturally, she is enraged. If she is incompetent, she should have been fired 13 or 14 years ago; it seems exceedingly odd that only now should anyone discover her inadequacies. But she has nowhere to go with her problem.

By this time, campus women are ripe for paranoia of the most advanced type. True, all the terminations have been legitimate within the letter of the college statutes and the AAUP guidelines, and many of the women have been only marginally competent, but together the firings are beginning to form a pattern. And it is obvious, too, that even the most incompetent and alcoholic of males will not be threatened by this pattern. Disturbed, the women begin to raise the matter in informal meetings and at parties.

Naturally, faculty men, chairmen, and deans are infuriated by this questioning of their judgment. "I'd be the last person in the world to penalize a competent woman," says Hebe's chairman over cocktails. "I doubt, though, that there's a competent woman on this campus. We've always had a merit system. If these women were any good, they'd have been rewarded and they wouldn't have anything to complain about." He is asked how he has determined that

Hebe is less competent than her male peers. "Oh, someone would have thought to hire her full-time by now if she'd been any good." Not that they have ever done it this way, he admits. But they would. "Women—bullshit," says Penelope's dean. "Where were they when us guys were marching with the blacks back in the 1960's. Bullshit. I'm no bigot. But don't tell me I gotta worry about women when I already got blacks coming out of my ears." Muses another dean: "I like Circe. She's got nice tits. But Penelope? Who needs to worry about her?" Says still another dean: "There's no way I'm going to take jobs or money from a man—any man—to give to a woman."

Another woman, having expressed sympathy for one of these victims, is dressed down openly and viciously by her chairman, who considers her sympathy to be personal disloyalty to him. As an older woman, she has never been conscious of discrimination until now, but she realizes that the chairman would never have staged such a scene with a man of her rank. She broods and joins the women's caucus of her professional association. Several other women formally discuss the growing ferment with a "friendly" administrator. "Don't you girls worry about anything," he assures them. "We're going to look after you girls." One of his listeners, an older and distinguished full professor, is radicalized on the spot by the man's choice of words.

3. From Grievance to Mutiny

Although the storm clouds have gathered, there is often a long, sullen lull between resentments and publicization or legal action. The women now are meeting for lunch or supper; they are gathering in each other's living rooms to express their anxiety. Nonetheless, many of them still want to work within the established system. All they are asking at this point is that their male colleagues be dragged, kicking and screaming if necessary, into the ethical climate of, say, the late nineteenth century. Instead, they receive a new brochure on Affirmative Action, profusely illustrated with pictures of black and chicano men working side by side with white males. And they hear unconvincing expressions of sympathy. Georgina M. Smith describes what happened at Rutgers, even after a survey had shown the existence of discrimination: "University officials responded with expressions of grave concern, urging deans, directors, and department chairmen to avoid discrimination in recruiting, hiring, and promotions. In the view of women faculty, the sentiments expressed were praiseworthy, but their practical effect was well-nigh invisible." [11]

More likely, communication between administrators and women—even between male faculty members and women—is cut off, often inadvertently. Says an administrator: "Gee, I used to like working with good old Hepzibah, but since she's gotten involved in all that stuff about women, she can't talk about anything except how low women's salaries are whenever the salary committee meets. I guess we'd better get her off that committee." A male acquaintance is quick to carry back this tidbit to good old Hepzibah, who naturally sees that as evidence of malevolent Watergate mentalities: "Don't solve a problem. Bury it." Simultaneously, other male administrators and faculty are reinforcing their collective machismo with boozy luncheons at the faculty club. Without intending to, they urge each other on to a campaign of harassment, repression, and name-calling, just as the women are similarly reinforcing each other's paranoia with similar meetings somewhere across town. The result farcically resembles a children's dance class. Boys are lined against one wall, girls against the other—only this time they are glaring at each other in the name of academic respectability and merit.

From this strained atmosphere, feminist leaders arise. Kay Klotzburger has provided a profile of leaders at the national level which, within certain limitations, seems also to describe women on individual campuses. The "advisory" leader—the type of woman who might be appointed to the women's committee of a national professional organization—is well over 30 and is not a specialist in women's studies. She holds an excellent degree (of course, this is unlikely to be true on any given campus), and she is a tenured associate or full professor. She publishes. She has never considered herself a feminist. The "activist" leader is a little younger; graduate of a good school, she may be an untenured member of the junior staff. Although her degree is not in women's studies, she may have developed a serious intellectual interest in the field.[12]

On individual campuses, the older "advisory" leader rises to prominence as the result of some crisis. Some are radicalized by the administration and senior male faculty —inadvertently, of course. Medea, for example, is safely tenured and interested only in her own scholarly future until, made curious by the female ferment, she wanders into her chairman's office to inquire why her salary is lower than might be expected. The result may be a veritable orgy of name-calling—she is a "paranoid," she is "greedy"—and Medea's anger is aroused. As we have seen, she is not easily mollified. Another, similar woman may step in to defend a more vulnerable, younger woman, only to discover that her opinion counts for nothing at all, even after many years of service. The result is another convert to the cause, although the woman had previously held aloof from lesser breeds outside the law.

Most unexpected is the reaction of the older and more prestigious woman who experiences her first soul-searching on the subject when she is appointed to serve on a campus Affirmative Action committee; having never questioned the self-proclaimed academic values, she now has the moral squalor of campus politics thrust into her face for the first time. It is made clear that the committee will not be allowed any significant information, that its function is to support the administration, that the whole thing is no more than window dressing. The woman becomes aware that she has been appointed solely because she is considered least likely to rock the boat. For the woman of integrity, this is insulting, and she will inevitably remember how many other such insults she has passively endured. What happens to her may strangely resemble religious conversion. Painfully, she discovers what Bernard Shaw knew when he wrote that "the only real tragedy in life is the being used by personally minded men for purposes which you recognize to be base." [13] Her conversion is dramatic and there will be no turning back.

Younger, "activist" women generally have no access to the power structure. As ferment increases, they get to know each other by chatting about pay scale and tenure denials in the restrooms and in the corridors. As untenured faculty, the dangers are very real to them, and men do much to reinforce their fears. Said a faculty man to a woman Ph.D., anxiously awaiting a tenure decision: "Don't'worry. Women shouldn't ever go beyond the master's degree anyhow. That's all my wife has." Younger women, too, have more informal contact with women students and will receive the students' confidences and complaints. When, year after year, students who do not even know each other complain that "Professor Lovelace keeps insisting I go to bed with him before he'll give me my grade," or "Professor Juniper was so drunk the other day that he walked right into the classroom and took hold of my breasts in front of everybody," the teacher will realize that some of these complaints ought to be taken seriously —and are not. It is much easier to fire Hebe and Penelope than to ask embarrassing questions about male competence and behavior.

Either heartsick or bitter, the activist may try to start a caucus. (If she does not, some older woman may step in and do it for her, for, after verbal communication has been cut off—except for occasional insults—the organization of an active caucus is the last warning flare that the responsible women can send up and it offers a chance for formalized participation by members of the caucus in Affirmative Action planning and implementation.) As everyone knows, caucuses are problematical. They are effective in national professional organizations or in institutions large enough to have a substantial number of women who share common needs, disciplines, and ideas. Caroline Bird, in fact, cites a study by Lucy Sells in which a caucus is held responsible for a dramatic decline in dropout rates for women graduate students in sociology at the University of California, Berkeley.[14] Obviously, though, one cannot form a caucus of the three women in the history department of Gopher's Gulch State College, and, where one must reach across campus for a heterogeneous mix of ages, skills, intelligences, and interests, the caucus is almost guaranteed to self-destruct as a function of the (largely male-conditioned) intolerance of women for each other. But, in desperation, the women try.

By this time, however, several women will be negotiating with lawyers, either because of termination or of salary, to which attention has by now been drawn. Usually, university salaries are difficult to ascertain and to discuss them is considered a violation of professional etiquette. By now, however, the women will have thrown away the rulebook. By crossing those techniques of research learned in graduate schools with methods of espionage gleaned from newspaper headlines and writings on the Second World War, it is usually possible to locate the information, while it is much more difficult to get a firm hold on the nebulous issues of promotion and retention. By now, too, some area lawyer is actively encouraging prospective clients, and he too wants nice, tangible issues such as salary.

Now everybody loses. The women have been snubbed and insulted until even the most conservative cannot ignore it. Hurt beyond measure, many fall back on a scattergun technique. If Medea works through the president's office, Circe exploits the public press, while Penelope goes to the Wage and Hour people, and Hebe contacts HEW. Hepzibah will be writing a state employment commission, and someone else may very well be writing the President of the United States. These efforts are designed to attract public notice, for the women have justifiably concluded that nothing short of cataclysm will help resolve their problems. And they want, too, to hit back.

Now, at the worst possible moment, something breaks into the headlines. In the campus newspaper and the public media, the women sound like spiritual descendants of Carrie Nation and Lizzie Borden, apt to burn bras and abort themselves on any street corner. Administrators, still helplessly incapable of admitting an error, are monotonously repeating that they are the best of all possible administrators on the best of all campuses, in the best of all possible worlds. To an audience educated by Watergate, there is something here that lacks credibility; besides, the administrative voices are weakening and they do not sound like they believe their own arguments any more. Faculty males, on the other hand, are just getting their second wind. Deliberately oblivious to all that has gone before, they now see that the central issue is salary and assume that the money given to women is being stolen from their own pockets. The president of a college who moves to resolve female grievances will now be in serious trouble with the male faculty. Many faculty men, who recently denounced the Watergate ethos with its assumption that politicians are above the law, are now quick to denounce government intervention into academic affairs—academics, clearly, are beyond the law themselves. And, now, students will be affected. As early as 1959, Dean William Storrs Lee brooded lest "the operation of the college itself" offer students no "very inspiring example of integrity." [15] He was rightfully alarmed, for the current student disenchantment with academic pretensions is partly the fault of those academics who, when tested, prove no more scrupulous than the greediest of industrialists. Especially hard hit will be those areas, such as the humanities, which have traditionally been dependent on a predominantly female undergraduate enrollment. English Departments, for example, fall into this classification, and because these departments have traditionally hired and underpaid their female faculty, they are now faced with a flood of charges of discrimination. Young women students turn away, rejecting the entire discipline because of the behavior of a few of its professors. That attitude may be adolescent in its exaggerations, but it is hard to refute the students' arguments that, so far as they can see, the discipline offers little opportunity for them.

8

Treading the Waters of Oblivion

For various reasons, many educational institutions remain immune to feminist agitation. And even where government investigations and litigation have occurred, women often discover that their trust in Big Brother or Uncle Sam has been touchingly childlike—a faint, weary echo of some infantile faith in God or human parent as *deus ex machina,* and one leading to the same disillusionment. Something similar often happens where women place their faith in collective bargaining, another popular panacea of the moment. Despite some immediate gains, women survive to experience a backlash that is quick and brutal. After that too dies down, the survivors, like their less activist sisters at more cloistered institutions, find themselves back on a treadmill. Ironically, their rebellion against the tedious domesticity of their parents' homes leads them, at the cost of much money, time, and pain, only to another kind of monotonous routine. And since few people behave quite rationally when deprived of all hope, it is not surprising that childhood emotions, habits, and modes of coping with frustration should surge back from where they have been buried not too deeply below the level of consciousness to create behavioral patterns that make the women burdensome to their colleagues and to themselves.

At those schools that have suffered through an active feminist movement, male backlash has long-range and disheartening consequences. Long ago, Caplow and McGee observed that political involvement is suspect in academe and is enough to hinder professional advancement.[1] Feminist involvement, however clearly it may be focused on problems of immediate economic survival, is automatically interpreted in the light of radical politics, sometimes with the unwitting assistance of the women themselves who, in their increasing frustration, allow themselves to fall into the exaggerations of revolutionary rhetoric. Because it is in their interest to do so, male colleagues will recall only the more antic performances, concluding, albeit illogically, that all are a "bunch of dumb broads" who want to devote their biology courses to seminars on "How to Castrate Male Rapists." Because this is what they want to believe and because academics rarely analyze their own motives or behavior, the males will be so certain of the reasonableness of their position that no impartial survey or court findings will be allowed to influence their judgments.

And, once justified in their own minds, males will take their revenge. Junior faculty activists, who have published a bit more about female sexuality than about the rectal temperatures of Alaskan seals, will find themselves denied tenure; their fellow biologists judge their publications to be "frivolous" and "unprofessional." Older women lose whatever status they have painfully acquired. Once labelled "feminist," the woman's every statement will be greeted with elegantly raised eyebrows or fine ironic academic smiles, while somewhere across the room one man whispers to another: "I wonder if she's burned any bras lately." Almost vindictively, some men take new delight in hiring Penelopes and Hebes in even greater numbers, especially as temporary or part-time employees. In doing so, the men are making two points. First, since these women are almost guaranteed to be relatively incompetent, the men will again point to their inadequacies as further evidence of female mindlessness and general inadequacy— and this time they will have made sure that the women can make no other kind of case for themselves. Second, they are collecting evidence of their own sometimes doubtful virility by showing that neither HEW nor lawyers nor activists can keep them, as certified he-men, from continuing to use women as cannon fodder.

At some schools, disillusionment is palpable among women who have been cajoled into supporting collective bargaining. Bribed with promises of equity, they have found that, once unions are accepted, nothing much happens except a consolidation of the status quo. Salary may be raised slightly and sometimes promotion policies are regularized, but the problems of temporary, part-time, and other exotic appointments remain. Women may still be used as cannon fodder, and they may be no more welcome in the academic unions than they have been in the past among plumbers, carpenters, and teamsters.

Most women, then, retire to a life of quiet desperation, watching, often with increasing bitterness, as young men are hired, promoted, paid, escalated into administration, propelled outward into bigger and better jobs. As a general rule, a woman's salary now remains low, Affirmative Action principles notwithstanding, and she will spend more time in rank than will a man. In a study at Connecticut College, for example, it was learned that women spent more time in rank even though they were more likely to hold the doctorate at the time of appointment; they were a full four and a half years behind men in being promoted to full professor.[2]

Middle-age is a fruitful period for only a few. The dedicated woman scholar may just be hitting her stride in those years. Having determined to outpublish her colleagues at all cost (no difficult matter on many campuses), she is not frustrated by the need to work alone or by the lack of reinforcement from her colleagues. But in some areas the chances of publication may be diminishing. In a study of publication among members of the Modern Language Association, Caroline D. Eckhardt and John B. Smith found that, statistically, the "easiest" years to have obtained a publishing commitment were in 1962, 1963, and 1970. Now, they find, university presses report "overpublishing" in such areas as literary criticism, since, as one correspondent phrased it, "a good deal of sawdust was put between hard covers" in the "balmy days" of the last decade.[3] But even the best and most-published of women scholars may also become discouraged. Neither on individual campuses nor at national meetings are women scholars admitted freely to those gatherings where the old boys meet to stroke each other. Credentials are rarely seen, reputation too often rests only on rumor, and there is nobody, usually, to speak for her. Even on her own campus, when it is learned that she has been asked to present a paper, chair a meeting, or service as consultant, the news will be received in the faculty club with not-too-polite astonishment. At the announcement of a book, someone will snicker: "After all, it's only her dissertation, and you know her adviser must have written most of *that*." Twenty years later, no matter what she has accomplished, someone still will be shaking his head and muttering: "Shallow. Very, very shallow."

Much the same kind of discouragement may affect the handful of women who have entered administration. Most women administrators do not enter from the teaching ranks. These "administrative assistants" or deans of women are veteran counselors or guidance experts, and they do not find themselves on the level where significant decisions are made. In a study at Purdue University, 215 women and 527 men were found to be classed in administrative positions, but 43 of the women were listed as administrative officers, many of them serving in resident-hall kitchens, while the rest were administrative assistants, a title often given to office workers as a reward for long years of service.[4] The age-old arguments arise with monotonous regularity whenever women are considered for more important positions: Will a woman be comfortable at meetings where men curse? (Any good medievalist or Renaissance scholar will have acquired a rich, full variety of obscenities with which she could challenge any academic personnel man.) Would men take orders from women? (If it is clear that they must, yes.) Who will pick up the check when she takes a visiting dignitary to a restaurant? (A trivial problem, surely.)

Thus, as she ages, the woman is increasingly dependent

for status on teaching; she has no other hopes left. Yet teaching is the one activity that carries no status, for no one is quite certain what teaching is. There is, of course, intense disagreement as to whether students are supposed to memorize facts, learn to handle ideas, learn to master technical tools, or simply masturbate their egos. Since no one quite knows what the student is supposed to learn, no one, including most students, has any way of telling when the student has learned something. Hence, the academic community has fallen back on intrinsically ridiculous systems of evaluation.

One favorite, for example, has more to do with machismo than with pedagogy. According to this system, teaching merit can be judged by counting the number of students who are flunked. The weak teacher is the one who has no standards, and most of his students pass his courses; the strong teacher is exacting, and his students flunk. Obviously, it is far easier to fail students than to devote time to tutoring them, and this system tends to reward those who exert the least energy in their teaching, although it should be obvious that the successful teaching of, say, writing, can only be measured by the number of students who have learned to write. As it is, the teacher may be most rewarded when hordes of his students remain illiterate. Yet the system remains operative in many places, and the person who rejects it is accused of "mothering." The female term is used pejoratively and deliberately, for the academic "nurturant" has tended to be female. Debarred from recognition as a scholar or administrator and from the greatest share of graduate instruction and research, the woman has had more time to give to her students, and she has given them this time if only to keep her own mind or her ego alive. The result is that dedicated teaching has become a "female" activity of low status. Male faculty, in its collective fear of appearing effeminate, is quick to mock the "nurturant" teacher. It is committed to a "masculine" system that may also be demonstrably ineffective.

At the opposite extreme of silliness is that system by which rewards—promotions, tenure, and salary raises—are based almost exclusively on student evaluations. Where this system operates, rewards are handed out to Best Ham Actors of the Year—some of whom are not above pleading with their students for good evaluations, lest their wives and children starve. While this thespian school of teaching probably does little harm in certain fields, such as education, it is inconceivably damaging in such fields as physics and chemistry, for the most popular performers among the faculty may well be lecturing from graduate notes that were last revised and updated in 1935. Nevertheless, women have much to gain from this system. Frequently, as in the case of Medea, their verbal histrionics pay off. Often too the classroom is the only arena in which a woman is free to display her personality at its best. (To be fair, this is also true for a few men.) Some women also use teaching much as certain actors use their stage parts—as vehicles for displaying the traits they only wished they possessed. In his survey of *The Girls on the Campus*, Jack Olsen presents one such woman.[5] His "Ingeborg Engemark," a 42-year-old assistant professor of English, obviously discards her own troubled personality as she enters the classroom door. In front of her students, she projects toughness, decisiveness, autonomy, while her private character is governed by a pathetic insecurity. She is an alcoholic; her frustrated sexuality is too easily exploited; her need for acceptance and affection are crippling in her professional life and oppressive to her friends.

Unfortunately, she is not untypical, for the occasional chance to gain ego-reinforcement or rewards through classroom performance is simply not enough. The mere boredom and frustration of interminable routine, empty of any hope for the future, is enough to bring out the worst in anyone. Thus, even after students and subject matter have been sacrificed to the instructor's therapy, the therapy itself fails, and no one gains much from the system.

If we take Medea, for example, it is almost literally true that, as Bernard Shaw wrote, "There is a point at which tedium becomes homicidal mania." [6] In her mid-Victorian tract on *Characteristics of Women*, Anna Jameson, describing Paulina in Shakespeare's *Winter's Tale*, presents an almost flawless sketch of this type of personality as it appears in its maturity:

She is . . . a clever, generous, strong-minded, warm-hearted woman, fearless in asserting the truth, firm in her sense of right, enthusiastic in all her affections: quick in thought, resolute in word, and energetic in action; but heedless, hot-tempered, impatient, loud, bold, voluble, and turbulent of tongue; regardless of the feelings of those for whom she would sacrifice her life, and injuring from excess of zeal those whom she most wishes to serve. [7]

"How many such there are in the world," muses Mrs. Jameson, and she is quite right. Unfortunately, the potentiality for generosity and warmth in Medea has never had a chance for development. Phrased bluntly, Medea is becoming an egomaniac; she listens to no one. Indeed, there is no way to attract her attention or to interrupt her monologues short of physical assault.

From childhood, Medea has wanted status and recognition. At about 45, she realizes that they will never come—not even the recognition her publications would normally attract if she were a man. No matter how hard she tries, there are no rewards. The hostility boils within her until, after a while, there is no conceivable reward that could calm her turbulent sense of injustice. Often her students praise her, but she is far from pleased at that, for she realizes that this kind of excellence is held in low esteem by her male colleagues, and it is their approbation that she craves. She still wants to be one of the boys. And so she keeps talking, hoping against hope that, if she talks long enough, her merits will finally be perceived.

In the privacy of her study, Medea broods over administrators, to whom she is exceedingly hostile. She is convinced she could do their jobs better than they, and once she would have been right. She knows, correctly, that she may collapse if she is doomed to another score of years in the same old classroom, teaching the same three or four subjects, for she dreads the start of each new term and the sight of each new face. Teaching basic college courses requires an assembly-line mentality, if it is to be accomplished by the men's rules, and Medea is both too bright and too energetic for this. At some schools, she will not even control the material she teaches. A chairman or committee will have designed the course, chosen the text, and set standards for examinations, and deviation from any of these will be considered a serious offense. But by the time Medea is middle-aged, her increasing insensitivity to the needs of others and her obliviousness to the sound of any voice except her own disqualify her from even the most trivial of administrative appointments. Medea naturally has no way of perceiving this. In her jealousy, she may well set out to make life miserable for her chairman or for the college president; she sees the baiting of administrators as a public service. They see it as a consequence of menopause.

Similarly, she may play power games within the department, gathering to her bosom whatever disciples are available—colorless, spineless newcomers usually, who are impressed by her publication record and who at first tend to believe that she is as important as she claims. She invites them to parties at her home, and the young, sorely tried by problems of adjustment and by the snobbishness of most of the senior staff, eventually warm to her and confide in her—as they do with the senior men who play this game, for it is a common academic game played by losers of any sex. These confidences give her something new to talk about, her colleagues having become bored long ago with her other verbal routines. When poor, vulnerable Hebe whispers of an affair with Professor Chowderhead, Medea thoughtlessly spreads the news, and Professor Chowderhead's wife sees to it that Hebe's job is terminated at the end of the year. When a young and transcendently inept hustler yearns to reform the department, Medea listens and nods sympathetically, while to her colleagues she spreads the word that young Borgia's getting too big for his breeches; and for once the senior men listen attentively, for they greatly fear those hungry generations treading them down. Medea of course has no sense of what she has done, even when Hebe and Borgia return to her, limping and wailing. She is dumbfounded by their complaints and wounded by their ingratitude, for not every senior professor would have given youngsters so much time and attention. She is completely unaware of the sense of power that she enjoys in finding and telling their secrets, and she will swear that nothing she has done was solely for the gratification of her own ego.

Ultimately, Medea is a tragic figure, her psyche a battleground of warring emotions. Within a decade or two, her colleagues, one by one, will learn to avoid her, and even the young will be warned away. No one will perceive that tragedy lies in the need of such a woman, bright as she is, to seek ego rewards in such nonsense. But there is no way of stopping the game at this point. As she paces out the dreary years toward retirement, she will hardly grow more rational. Increasingly ostracized, she will accuse her colleagues of hiding her mail, of concealing information, of holding meetings only when she is tied up in class. Sometimes, desperate for attention, she goes so far as to accuse students or colleagues of stealing research material from her office (she left it in the car) or her keys from her purse (they are in her coat pocket) and the departmental budget is depleted by her repeated demands that the lock on her office door be changed. Her frustrated desire for esteem has fizzled out in the mere need to be the center of attention, which she manages by behavior strangely reminiscent of the tantrums of her infancy.

Circe, too, joins the ranks of the walking wounded, provided she survives the tenure decision at all. Now her problem will be that age and custom wither and stale her very finite variety. The sag of once-firm breasts, the first hint of a triple-chin, the suggestion of a pot-belly—nothing has prepared Circe to cope with all this. Occasionally a miracle happens. Circe, aware that something is going wrong, settles down to a lengthy period of introspection, emerging as a professionally competent teacher and an active researcher. More often, she does what most people do. When in doubt, she does the same things she has been doing, only more so. But by now her bobbing breasts—the same old breasts, day after day—have become a bit of a bore, especially on a college campus where a new crop of young, nubile flesh is brought to market yearly. Her colleagues no longer flirt with her. Instead they snicker. The students who once resented her laugh openly, and young boys never get crushes on her any more. The result is that she becomes more aggressive, like her country-club counterpart. And like these more fashionable women, Circe may actually begin to take lovers, if anyone is still interested. Probably no one is. When Circe discovers as much, she sometimes begins to haunt local bars, and when even here she can find no partner for her games, she becomes a prime candidate for a breakdown or, more probably, for that not uncommon academic disease: alcoholism.

Also, by the time she is 40 or 45, Circe's career is dead. Her professional credentials are depressing. When she complains, administrators, gently smirking, retort that *bars* do not have to pay certain kinds of women for working on the premises. Male colleagues are even more unsupportive than usual. If they genuinely possess any sense of academic merit, they look at her credentials and wonder why they gave her tenure. When, more normally, they make judgments subjectively and irrationally, they stereotype her as the "evil" seductress of American literature and folklore—and, besides, they are tired of Circe anyhow. And Circe receives little support from other women, even

now when she has become pathetic. Dowdy little colleagues resent her earlier successes at sexual games-play-
ing, for they have never been equipped to compete in
what once was Circe's world. Medusa the drudge will be
envious, because Circe got almost as far as she did without even trying. Genuine scholars like Medea are contemptuous. Those other women, some of them feminists,
who are concerned with honesty and integrity, with the
abandonment of infantile sexual games, and with fair deal-
ing between sexes, will pity Circe—but they will also
loathe her. She gives women—and sometimes feminism—
a bad name. In short, Circe stands alone, which is the role
of all roles that she is least fitted for.

Medusa, too, granulates away. By the time she is 40 she
is irrevocably a dreary little person with long skirts, support hose, and tennis shoes. She is content with the crumbs
from her colleagues' tables, with the rottenest schedules
at the worst hours, and she willingly supervises student
teachers and oversees the school newspaper as an over-
load. Her colleagues tend to forget she exists, except when
there is scutwork to do, and, as she is never called on to
use her brain, it begins manifestly to atrophy. Sometimes,
at about 40 or 45, she succumbs to housewife's lament:
the years have gone by, she is aging, she has done nothing
of any significance. In the privacy of her apartment, she
begins to sip blackberry brandy or cooking sherry. When
this goes on too long, she may succumb to deep and overwhelming depression which she may end by driving her
car into a telephone pole. A few such women, however,
are eventually affected by recent feminist activity, and
when this happens Medusa releases the profound anger
long suppressed. She sends off letters to newspaper editors,

to government agencies, to university administrators. They will not be able to solve her problems even if they wanted to, for her anger affects her prose style, and only rarely is anyone, including Medusa, quite certain of what it is that she wants. Her colleagues will be amused, and they will make wisecracks about menopause, except for the few who insist: "That's what happens when a woman doesn't get married and settle down."

As for Penelope and Hebe, they will probably bounce from job to job. If Penelope does not startle everyone by drifting into a noisy and public affair with one of her colleagues, she may drift into the game that Eric Berne calls "Harried." [8] If she is married, she can simultaneously play it at home as well. She takes on more and more work; her energies and interests cannot be satisfied by the piddling chores assigned to her—and the conditioning by which women are encouraged to volunteer for new chores operates here. Penelope never learns to abandon the piddling chores for some single, major effort; she never develops a professional's ability to focus on a single task and to do it well. Instead she believes that, while one piddling chore does not satisfy her, 10 or 12 of them will. Indeed, her "feminine" orientation causes her to deny her professionalism at every step of the way, either explicitly or by totally inappropriate chatter concerning her children, her groceries, or her womb in every inappropriate professional situation. Even when she has turned feminist, she will utter the same banalities. In between leading student marchers, she will still chatter about her children, her groceries, and her womb, only this time she does it ostensibly for the sake of giving recognition to "feminine" functions—to the "sensitive, intuitive, emotional," and so on.

Hebe's real life rarely occurs on campus. So long as her body holds out, she may still serve the community as she did in her girlhood, and her home may be a haven for every drug freak and crasher in her geographic vicinity, which may ultimately involve her with the police and get her fired. Somewhat more acceptably she may turn, as she ages, to one of the less rational religious movements, and may achieve a certain measure of stability by dedicating her efforts to God or to meditation, possibly under the direction of a faculty guru of which there is never any shortage. The guru, usually a considerably older man, will need a befuddled female disciple just as badly as Hebe needs someone to serve. Originally, if the man is a sociologist or psychologist, he may have justified the relationship by stating his intentions of aiding Hebe, but actually no improvement will be effected; they need each other too much just as they are. In these relationships, there is a quality unpleasantly reminiscent of the relationship between a procurer and his whore, for Hebe must continue to run around doing dumb things so that her mentor can calm her and control her. The relationship may be perfectly chaste; Hebe's dependency may never affect her mentor's marriage. And if the guru is politically powerful, Hebe may stay around for a number of years. If he is very powerful, she may be tenured.

It must be remembered that these figures are stereotypes, not real people. But all campuses have women who are troubled, and troubled in some of the ways suggested above. And when troubled women enter into a profession that itself teems with absurdities, the only possible result is more trouble, both for the profession and for the individual. But the women's troubles are inevitably interpreted as failures—not of the system, but of the women. By thus interpreting them, men find justification for newer and more lunatic orgies of chauvinism, with the result that the next generation of women may be even more disastrously educated than was the last one.

9

Toward a More
Promising Future

The present problems of women in higher education are
a result in part of staggering, but correctable, failures
within the system itself. Most conspicuous among these is
the failure of even academic historians, sociologists, and
political scientists to acknowledge the fact that the life of
women is changing, and has been for the last century, and
that this change may have serious consequences in education. Too often even sociologists prefer to believe that
all blacks reside in unspeakable ghettoes and that women
are eternally unchanged, except that, thanks to the pill,
the poor creatures are much more promiscuous than they
used to be. But almost a century ago Thorstein Veblen
warned that what was traditionally considered the "good
and natural" role for women was already outliving its social usefulness, no longer serving the "more everyday ends
of life in a modern industrial community." Veblen wrote:

Even that large and substantial body of well-bred, upper and middle-class women to whose dispassionate, matronly sense of the traditional proprieties this [conventional role] commends itself as fundamentally and eternally right—even these, whose attitude is conservative, commonly find some slight discrepancy in detail between things as they are and things as they should be. . . . But that less manageable body of modern women who, by force of youth, education, or temperament, are in some degree out of touch with the traditions of status received from the barbarian culture, and in whom there is, perhaps, an undue reversion to the impulse of self-expression and work-manship—these are touched with a sense of grievance too vivid to leave them at rest.[1]

Despite periodic setbacks, as in the decade following the Second World War, women have been increasingly rest-less for the past century. And today there is about as much chance of getting them to return to their kitchen sinks and their dust mops as there is to coerce the middle-class black back to unpaid cotton-picking on the old plantation. It is the tragedy of the academic community that it wants to ignore all of this, while pretending to be the conservator of human wisdom and knowledge. For almost a century, academics ignored the Emancipation Proclamation and they were bitterly shocked when blacks, as tax-payers, de-manded access to state-supported schools and equity within them. Deliberately, academics misinterpreted each request for equity as a demand for egalitarianism (al-though the two are manifestly different) and complained that they would find themselves teaching mongoloids next, if this movement toward egalitarianism were not halted. The result, of course, was the black academic agitation of the 1960's. Just about the same thing is now happening with women.

Mercifully, feminist agitation coincides with a crisis of education which should make it relatively simple to attract faculty and administrative attention to the long-ignored female elements of the community. Presently, colleges and universities need students more than they need anything else, except perhaps money. Often it is the most intransigently conservative disciplines that are the most desperate, existing under the threat of faculty layoffs in the face of continually declining student enrollments. Many colleges have hired professional recruiters, paying so much a head for every new student brought into the fold. Naturally, this is self-defeating—or soon will be—for colleges are mostly grabbing 18-year-old bodies from each other, and all the while the pool of available 18-year-old bodies is steadily declining, while simultaneously junior and community college facilities are just as steadily expanding. Ultimately, it will be necessary to look toward a new pool of potential students.

The most obvious pool is that of half-educated women, many of them already employed as semi-skilled and distinctly underpaid labor. For them, education is not a luxury; it is necessary for sheer survival. They are kept away from the colleges by advisers contemptuous of older women returning to school, by professors who make wisecracks about little old ladies, by failures of child-care and scholarship programs to account for their needs, and by the failure of academic departments to schedule to meet the needs of a working populace. Much of this, of course, has been deliberate. Adult education carries with it the lowest status. But colleges and universities can no longer afford that kind of snobbishness, and faculties, in the name of that self-interest which can always be counted upon as motivation, can probably be brought around eventually.

Even among homebodies, increased life expectancy and decreased childbearing have resulted in a large number of potential students. As our society exists today, it is obvious that most women are confronted by the bleak prospect of idle decades, extending from the day their youngest child enters high school to the moment when, long widowed, they lie abandoned in an old folks' home. While it is ridiculous to assume that all housewives will cease to be housewives with passage of the Equal Rights Amendment, it is a reasonable assumption that many would prefer the mastery of art of philosophy or literature to a mastery of pill-popping and bed-hopping or even gardening, if only because the brain wears better, as a rule, than the body. Moreover, in the face of rising divorce rates, many women are now motivated to keep their minds alive —they never know when they will need to use them. And, too, some men and women just like to learn things. Universities, with their intolerant attitudes toward anyone not possessing or pursuing the Ph.D., have too long forgotten that knowledge can be pleasure and that the desire to know and to see clearly is at least as respectable a motive as the desire to acquire a Ph.D. and write learned, obscure articles.

But higher education has never welcomed women, except for the appropriately docile—and sexy—products of respectable, middle-class high schools. Female oddities have been fed into jerry-built continuing-education programs where they receive the worst possible instruction from the least qualified instructors—graduate students who are mostly interested in completing their degrees or, in some cases, whatever live bodies can be hired off street corners. Recently there has been a tendency to use the more shoddily constructed black and women's programs as similar dumping grounds. And even in community and junior colleges, there is little counselling, although older women and ugly or nonconformist young ones are often crippled by depression and by a sense of inadequacy, futility, or loneliness. Male academics, rejecting the "nurturing" role associated with counselling, find it easier to ridicule such students than to educate them. When forced to counsel, they fall back on banalities: "Why don't you go home and have more babies?" or "I don't see why women need an education" or "You'll be happy when you learn to be what Freud regards as a good woman." It is little wonder that women often drop out as casually as they have been allowed to drift in.

Thus, the matter that should have highest priority is the convincing of administrators that women are necessary to the survival of education, but that women cannot be recruited so long as the system remains chauvinistic and 18-year-old-oriented in all its aspects.

A somewhat more difficult problem will be to insist that feminist materials and subjects be used to revivify the stultified curricula in many of the traditional disciplines. Too often, feminists and chauvinists unwittingly cooperate to relegate such materials to women's studies programs when more properly they should be used to give new life to regular studies which have grown practically moribund.

With a certain amount of craftiness, however, men can be attacked on their own ground. In 1969 J. Douglas

Brown wrote that the function of liberal education is "to pursue self-education in things important to himself [sic] and not solely in preparation for the precise demands of a predetermined occupation." Moreover, the university must seek "to free men from ignorance, superstition, prejudice, arrogance, hatred, tyranny, greed, insensitivity, and cynicism and to strengthen their respect for the freedom and dignity of other free individuals in their self-fulfillment. . . ." [2] It may be argued that, so long as academic curricula are themselves based on superstition, hatred, ignorance, and prejudice, the liberal educators can do no more than ignominiously fail in these tasks. Too often literature students are yearly exposed to Ernest Hemingway until they are sick unto death of the man, while on the other hand even graduate students have never read Virginia Woolf or Flannery O'Connor, and a surprising number of them know of Austen and the Brontës only through passing references in survey courses. Too often, history students learn and relearn the intricacies of the Napoleonic campaigns, while eighteenth-century agricultural reforms with their demonstrable effects upon the lives of women and children remain a deep dark secret. Nor is it at all obvious why William Godwin is so much more important than Mary Wollstonecraft or why psychology must be only Skinner when it is not Freud. Or why so many studies of political reforms pay no attention whatever to parliamentary acts affecting married women's property or divorce or the legalization, in this country, of information concerning contraceptives, despite the fact that these bills revolutionized life for large portions of the population.

Such pointed selectivity is censorship and should be reproached as such. What is involved here is a basic matter of academic freedom. It would be a violation of the professor's freedom to insist that a Freudian professor of psychology change his ways, but it is an equal violation when only the Freudian perspective is permitted in a department of psychology or education.

Moreover, when fields such as English or history or political science reach out once more to touch on the world as it actually exists, knowledge again will become attractive. Just as it seems likely that Gay Lib has done much to create new interest in classical Greek studies, which are once more springing to life in the most unexpected places, so other disciplines will find that there is less need for active recruitment of students when a program has become intrinsically attractive.

Thus a second necessary step toward academic sanity is the integration of academic curricula.

It will be argued, of course, that professors presently teaching are not trained in such materials and will not know how to handle them. This is true. It illustrates the need to hire new and qualified women and it also shows the need to de-chauvinize the attitudes toward women presently teaching in colleges and universities. They are legitimate members of the faculty—or should be—and must be treated as such, if only because female students will not be attracted to departments in which the only female members of the faculty are hang-dogged, shame-faced, howling neurotics, with neither status, self-esteem, nor future. While one can do nothing to remedy, at this point, the problems of American girlhood that have made Circe and Medea what they are, one can at least ensure that they are made no worse by the problems of professional adulthood. These will always be troubled women, but to allow them to conceptualize themselves as professional and human is to do a service, not only to them, but to the students and to their colleagues, male and female alike. Allowed some measure of self-esteem, they will become more effective in attracting bright students, and they will be easier to work with for everyone concerned.

A third urgent step, then, is the brainwashing of male faculty and administration. They must be taught that not only the law is involved. It is in their own best interest to begin scuttling, not the women, but the values of the old boys network, treating fairly the women with whom they work and hiring as many others as are necessary to a fully integrated curriculum.

But academic women will not be able to feel pride in their profession until their own areas of expertise are properly valued. Scholarship, too, must reach out and touch the world as it actually exists; and, just as the woman should not be deprived of research time and funds because she is a woman, so should she not be deprived of them because her area of expertise involves women. There is no particularly good reason why the thousandth book about Rembrandt should be valued more highly than the first book about a previously undiscovered Gothic woman sculptor, nor is there any reason why one more in an endless series of notes on puns in Chaucer should be more precious than a work on the life of women in the Middle Ages, as reflected in the literature.

What is more, it is in the best interest of professors that they should learn to view matters in this way, for in their narrowness and arrogance professors in many fields are phasing themselves rapidly out of existence. There are too many scholarly works on too few subjects, as the remainder lists from academic publishing houses regularly suggest. In certain fields, formalism has too long dominated. Sociology, political science, history, anthropology, literature, philosophy—these are no more than the shaping of experience, but in their elitism most professors have come to concentrate on the shaping at the expense of the experience. Fortunately, significant voices are now urging a return to the basic issues. For example, in his Phi Beta Kappa Award-winning study of Bernard Shaw, Louis Crompton announces his own commitment to the tradition of "moral realism," and implicitly urges a return to this "classical tradition of English literary criticism . . . from Sir Philip Sidney down to Johnson, Shelley, and Ruskin. . . ."[3] He is rebelling, of course, against those New Critics who too often insist that literature be totally divorced from all philosophic, historical, or social context—in other words, from all that makes literature interesting to nine-tenths of the people who might read it. Similarly, Cambridge-educated Jacquetta Hawkes, in *The First Great Civilizations*, condemns the pedantry that reduces history to "technical problems of exceptional professional complexity but of small social importance."[4] Materials concerning women have much to offer in such fields, for the incorporation of any new mass of human materials offers the promise of new vigor.

It is necessary then that scholarship be deemed meritous according to its intellectual and rhetorical content, regardless of the sex of its subject. And this is for the benefit, not just of women, but of scholarship itself. The rediscovery of half the human race can be at least as significant a discovery as the translation of the Rosetta Stone.

None of this can be accomplished, however, until women abandon their commitment to the anarchy that too often overwhelms any efforts at organized sisterhood. Put any 30 academic women together and the result will be depressingly predictable. Medea plays Queen Bee; she has made it to where she is without any help, and she sees no reason why others should receive more help than she did. Hebe will take great delight in shocking Medea. Unhindered by any knowledge of either Marxism or capitalism, she insists that the group begin by marching on Washington with the intent of overthrowing the U.S. government. Someone else thinks equity will be achieved if everyone quits wearing make-up or shaving their thighs, which is enough to send the 50-year-olds scuttling for the doorway. The *coup de grâce* is administered by a bright young thing who thinks the academic world would be vastly improved if women went around stripped to the waist. The older women who have not already left now flee in near hysteria.

None of this is necessary. What is involved is the retention of the most self-destructive elements of early conditioning. Having been encouraged to be emotional, the women assume that unmitigated emotionalism is natural to the female and they reject the intellectual discipline necessary for even the simplest problem-solving, with the result that problems do not get solved. Having never been allowed into traditional social structures, they reject the notion of structure. And the result is that problems do not get priorized—a necessary first step toward solution—and that even the discussion of problems is allowed to drift aimlessly from point to point, so that vast amounts of time are consumed to no perceptible end. At best, some delegate goes forth to rant incoherently at male faculty and administrators—which, even to many of the women within the group, is no way to substantiate claims to intellectual equality and to the merit on which tenure, promotions, and raises should properly be based. Surely, there is nothing wrong with terrifying a man who cannot be approached in any other way, but if one is basing one's claims on intellectual ability, it is best at least to begin with the assumption that rational discourse might be possible. It sometimes is.

Further, women are acculturated to accept second or third best. This bit of conditioning too is retained. By now, with the black precedent clearly before them, women should be wary of allowing themselves to be bought off with cheaply constructed women's courses and programs. Unless these are staffed with first-rate scholars, unless they are closely affiliated with traditional disciplinary programs, and unless there is a long-range fiscal commitment and careful scrutiny of course offerings, they too often have the potential of turning into academic garbage pits, and they will fail as so many black studies programs are now failing. Never, under any circumstances, should they be permitted as a substitute for integration of the regular curriculum. Never should they be staffed with the "temporary" or part-time help which automatically denotes low academic status.

Also many women retain a blind faith in the separateness of "feminine" activities, faith that ultimately does much to hurt women's causes. True, consciousness-raising is necessary for women, as for blacks. But not in the classroom. A 36-hour program in women's consciousness will do nothing to prepare the professionals that are so badly needed. Actual as opposed to apparent power rests in the hands of doctors, lawyers, engineers, politicians, and the rest. So long as physicians are mostly male, women will receive barbarically chauvinistic medical treatment, whether the prevailing economy be capitalist, communist, or socialist. And on the whole most women patients ultimately prefer a doctor who knows what organ she is cutting into to one who is noteworthy only for her heightened consciousness. In other words, women's studies can be exploited by the most intransigent chauvinists as a convenient method for keeping women out of precisely those programs in which they are most needed—and out of professions critically in need of reform. And feminists assist the chauvinists in doing this.

Again, far too much academic attention can be given to the current cant about the "intuitive," "sensitive," "irrational" female soul. Surely, no woman who works within an academic community can believe in the rationality of the male mind, as opposed to the irrationality of the female. Nothing can be more irrational than the ways in which male professors discern the intellectual merits of their colleagues, and nothing can be more irrational than the ways in which male physicians are trained to diagnose their female patients. Irrationality survives quite nicely in both sexes, without special cultivation. For women there is the danger that this preoccupation with their own sensitivity and irrationality will cause them to reject participation in the highly developed technology with which their freedom is inextricably bound. For women the gravest danger is that there will not be enough technology. Starvation, disease, high infant and maternal mortality, dangerous or non-existent contraceptive techniques, undiagnosed and untreated cervical cancers—these still are too prevalent. And it is clear that male professionals will never be concerned enough to deal with them adequately. Nor can females, until they are properly trained and prepared to accept, not flee, the intellectual discipline required in many of the scientific and technological fields.

This preoccupation with the peculiarly irrational nature of the female also poses certain other barriers to female advances, for too many feminists of this school insist that all women are infinitely lovable just as they are. Yet it is senseless to insist that men admire Medea, when the women cannot stand her themselves. It is useless to claim that Medusa is adorable when even feminists become depressed in the vicinity of this type of loser and will not spare enough time to patch together her threadbare ego. Again what are necessary are professionals, this time in education. There is need for a new kind of teacher and, above all, for a new kind of principal and school superintendent. Only then will it be possible to reward the bright girl and to encourage her to conceptualize herself as an individual, with a wide variety of choices among life styles and occupations. Something could be done about the more self-destructive traits of Hebe and of Circe while they are yet children, but only if it is admitted that women can be as damaged and as imperfect as are men and that behavior modification may be as necessary for the one sex as for the other.

So long as academic women continue to muddle their way into ineffectiveness, academic men will find it possible to cling to their atavistic biases and to support them in the community at large. Similarly, only when feminists acknowledge, however reluctantly, that they are irrevocably involved in a human community containing all manner of races and sexes and talents, will they turn their full and most efficient attentions to obtaining full participation in occupations which can influence the ideas—and use of technology—within that community. And it is possible, at this particular point in time, to make a good start by insisting that the academic community lead the way in attacking irrational prejudices, not wallowing in them.

Notes

INTRODUCTION

1. George Bernard Shaw, "Maxims for Revolutionists," in *Man and Superman: A Comedy and a Philosophy* (Baltimore: 1952), p. 262. There will be an unusually large number of often unnecessary footnotes in this book. I have noticed a tendency among male academics to dismiss all works of this type as the free-floating fantasies of female paranoics. Consequently, with sardonic and even malevolent forethought, I have introduced documentation and scholarly apparatus on every possible occasion.

2. "Affirmative Action for Women in 1971: A Report of the Modern Language Association Commission on the Status of Women in the Profession," *Publication of the Modern Language Association* 87 (May 1972), 531 and 538.

3. American Council on Education study reported in "The New Campus Rebels: Women," *Newsweek*, 82 (Dec. 10, 1973), 120.

4. Reported by Helen S. Astin and Alan E. Bayer, "Sex Discrimination in Academe," in *Academic Women on the Move*, ed. Alice S. Rossi and Ann Calderwood (New York: Russell Sage Foundation, 1973), p. 342.

5. There is not a shortage of data. Cf. especially Cynthia Fuchs Epstein, *Woman's Place: Options and Limits in Professional Careers* (Berkeley, Los Angeles, and London: University of California Press, 1971), pp. 8–9.

6. Caroline Bird, *Born Female: The High Cost of Keeping Women Down* (New York: Pocket Books, 1969), p. 83.

7. Katharine M. Rogers, *The Troublesome Helpmate: A History of Misogyny in Literature* (Seattle and London: University of Washington Press, 1966); Elizabeth Janeway, *Man's World, Woman's Place: A Study in Social Mythology* (New York: Dell, 1971); Judith Stacey, Susan Bereaud, and Joan Daniels, eds., *And Jill Came Tumbling After: Sexism in American Education* (New York: Dell, 1974); and Rossi and Calderwood, cited above.

8. Nancy Press Hawley, *et al.*, "Sexuality," *Our Bodies, Ourselves: A Book By and For Women*, by the Boston Women's Health Book Collective (New York: Simon & Schuster, 1973), p. 23.

9. Carolyn G. Heilbrun, *Toward a Recognition of Androgyny* (New York: Knopf, 1973).

10. Were this book not aimed at a scholarly audience, there would be no need to cite Virginia Woolf's famous tract, *A Room of One's Own* (New York: Harcourt Brace & World, 1929).

11. Cf. Karl Menninger's *Whatever Became of Sin?* (New York: Hawthorn Books, 1973).

CHAPTER 1. TWO PRESUPPOSITIONS CONCERNING CONDITIONING

1. Alix Kates Shulman, *Memoirs of an Ex-Prom Queen* (New York: Bantam Books, 1973), p. 74.

2. Simone Berteaut, *Piaf* (New York: Dell, 1973), p. 36.

3. Helen Gurley Brown, *Sex and the Single Girl* (New York: Pocket Books, 1963), p. 80.

4. Marcia Seligson, *The Eternal Bliss Machine: America's Way of Wedding* (New York: Morrow, 1973), p. 123.

5. Alice Rossi, "Discrimination and Demography Restrict Opportunities for Academic Women," in *And Jill Came Tumbling After*, cited above, p. 370.

6. U.S. Department of Commerce Bureau of the Census, *Statistical Abstract of the United States, 1973*, 94th ed., pp. 223 and 334; "California Employes on Welfare Rolls," *St. Louis Post-Dispatch* (April 14, 1974), p. 4B.

7. Cf. Joseph Campbell, *Myths to Live By* (New York: Viking, 1972), pp. 42 and 33.

8. George F. Gilder, *Sexual Suicide* (Cleveland: Quadrangle, 1973).

9. Anita Leslie, *The Marborough House Set* (New York: Doubleday, 1973); Elinor Glyn, *The Visits of Elizabeth* (London [Duckworth and Co.]: 1900); Cyril Pearl, *The Girl with the Swansdown Seat* (Indianapolis: Bobbs-Merrill, 1955); James Laver, *Manners and Morals in the Age of Optimism, 1848–1914* (New York and

Evanston: Harper & Row, 1966); Margaret Armstrong, *Fanny Kemble: A Passionate Victorian* (New York: Macmillan, 1938), and Kemble's own American memoirs, "A Residence on a Georgian Plantation," published in 1863; Elizabeth Drexel Lehr, *"King Lehr" and the Gilded Age, with Extracts from the Locked Diary of Harry Lehr* (Philadelphia: Lippincott, 1935), and Jonathan Gathorne-Hardy, *The Unnatural History of the Nanny* (New York: Dial Press, 1973).

10. The 1864 factory inspector's report is quoted by E. Royston Pike, ed., in *"Golden Times": Human Documents of the Victorian Age* (New York: Schocken Books, 1972), a book which also provides especially useful material on the lives and occupations of working-class women (cf. pp. 92–93). Other sources here include Laver, cited above, p. 86; and Jacob A. Riis, *How the Other Half Lives: Studies Among the Tenements of New York* (New York: Dover, 1971), a reprint of a work first published in 1890.

11. Leon Edel, *Henry James: The Conquest of London, 1870–1881* (Philadelphia and New York: Lippincott, 1962), pp. 50–51; Florence Nightingale, "Cassandra," privately published in 1859 and reprinted as an appendix to Ray Strachey's *"The Cause": A Short History of the Women's Movement in Great Britain* (London: G. Bell and Sons, 1928), pp. 395–418, esp. p. 410.

12. George Bernard Shaw, preface to *Mrs. Warren's Profession* in *Plays Unpleasant* (Baltimore: Penguin, 1961), p. 186.

13. For statistics on prostitution, see Pearl, pp. 36–37, William Acton, *Prostitution,* ed. Peter Fryer (New York: Praeger, 1969; first published in 1857); or E. M. Sigsworth and T. J. Wyke, "A Study of Victorian Prostitution and Venereal Disease," in *Suffer and Be Still: Women in the Victorian Age,* ed. Martha Vicinus (Bloomington, Ind.: Indiana University Press, 1972). Nineteenth-century statistics are usually little better than guesswork. The English are perhaps no more reliable than the American, but since it is obviously easier to summarize the tabulations of one relatively small country than to synthesize the sprawl of nineteenth-century America, a great deal of British material is being used here.

14. Kate Millett, *The Prostitute Papers: A Candid Dialogue* (New York: Avon, 1973), p. 55.

15. *The Autobiography of Mrs. Alice Thornton,* fragments of which are reprinted by Joan Goulianos, ed., in *By a Woman Writt: Literature from Six Centuries By and About Women* (Indianapolis: Bobbs-Merrill, 1973), p. 46.

16. Elizabeth Longford, *Queen Victoria: Born to Succeed* (New York: Pyramid, 1966), p. 234.

17. Quoted from *Country Magazine* (October 1736) by Alison

Adburgham in *Women in Print: Writing Women and Women's Magazines from the Restoration to the Accession of Queen Victoria* (London: George Allen & Unwin, 1972), p. 85.

18. G. M. Young, *Victorian England: Portrait of an Age* (London: Oxford University Press, 1960), p. 24.

19. Laver, p. 194.

20. Cecil Woodham-Smith, *Florence Nightingale* (New York: Avon, 1951), p. 307.

21. See pp. 203–213 of *Wicked Victorians: An Anthology of Clandestine Literature of the Nineteenth Century,* ed. Gordon Grimley (London: Odyssey, 1970).

CHAPTER 2. PREYING TOGETHER

1. Jane Howard, *A Different Woman* (New York: Dutton, 1973), p. 410.

2. Elinor Glyn, *The Philosophy of Love* (Auburn, N.Y.: Authors Press, 1923), p. 106.

3. Eric John Dingwall, *The American Woman: An Historical Study* (New York: Signet, 1958), p. 237.

4. Cf. Susan Goldberg and Michael Lewis, "Play Behavior in the Year-Old Infant," in *Readings on the Psychology of Women,* ed. Judith M. Bardwick (New York: Harper & Row, 1972), p. 30; Gary D. Mitchell, "Attachment Differences in Male and Female Infant Monkeys," also in Bardwick, p. 21.

5. Lillian Hellman, *An Unfinished Woman: A Memoir* (New York: Bantam, 1970), p. 5.

6. Ann Aldrich, "A Happy Life, A Constructive Life," in *Carol in a Thousand Cities* (Greenwich, Conn.: Fawcett, 1960), p. 227.

7. Jack Olsen, *The Girls in the Office* (New York: Pocket Books, 1973), p. 211.

8. Radclyffe Hall, *The Well of Loneliness* (Garden City, N.Y.: Sun Dial Press, 1928), p. 5.

9. Kitty Muggeridge and Ruth Adam, *Beatrice Webb: A Life, 1858–1943* (New York: Knopf, 1968), p. 20.

10. "The Death of Marilyn Monroe," in *Marilyn Monroe: A Composite View,* ed. Edward Wagenknecht (Philadelphia: Chilton, 1969), esp. p. 130.

11. Robert S. Lynd and Helen Merrell Lynd, *Middletown: A Study in American Culture* (New York: Harcourt Brace & World, 1956), p. 168.

12. Joanna Russ, "The Image of Women in Science Fiction," in *Images of Women in Fiction: Feminist Perspectives,* ed. Susan

Koppelman Cornillon (Bowling Green, O.: Bowling Green University Popular Press, 1972).

13. Howard Haycraft, *Murder for Pleasure: The Life and Times of the Detective Story* (New York: Biblo and Tanner, 1972), p. 230. First published, 1941.

14. Leopold Stein, *Anatomy of Eve* (New York: Popular Library, 1960), p. 132. Henry Blyth's *Caro, The Fatal Passion: The Life of Lady Caroline Lamb* is an excellent biography of one such type. Blyth is particularly attentive to the childhood circumstances that caused this volcanic Regency socialite to drive off her prime-minister husband (Lord Melbourne) and her poet lover (Lord Byron) by her volatile and assertive demands for attention and affection.

15. Clara M. Thompson, *On Women* (New York: New American Library, 1971), pp. 73–74.

CHAPTER 3. IN THE SCHOOLROOM

1. Samuel Butler, *Erewhon Revisited* (London: Page and Co., 1923), p. 155.

2. Margaret Mead, *Blackberry Winter: My Earlier Years* (New York: Morrow, 1972), p. 83.

3. Agnes de Mille, *Speak to Me, Dance With Me* (Boston: Little, Brown, 1973). Miss de Mille is granddaughter of Henry George, niece of Cecil B. de Mille, and these family figures may have had something to do with her intransigence.

4. Joseph P. Lash, *Eleanor and Franklin* (New York: New American Library, 1971), p. 74.

5. Fred Lawrence Guiles, *Norma Jean: The Life of Marilyn Monroe* (New York: Bantam, 1970), p. 20.

6. Cf. Ch. 2 of Hildegard Knef's *The Gift Horse*, tr. David A. Palastanga (New York: Dell, 1972).

7. Shulman, cited above, p. 52.

8. Sylvia Plath, *The Bell Jar* (New York: Bantam, 1972), p. 26.

9. Matina Horner, "The Motive to Avoid Success and Changing Aspirations of College Women," in Bardwick, previously cited, p. 64.

10. Grace K. Baruch, "Sex-Role Attitudes of Fifth-Grade Girls," in *And Jill Came Tumbling After*, pp. 199–200.

11. Eleanor Flexner, in *Century of Struggle: The Woman's Rights Movement in the United States* (New York: Atheneum, 1972), presents a terse, vivid account of early educational problems, many of which are relevant to this discussion. Cf. p. 30.

12. Quoted from *The Saturday Review* of September 12, 1857, by Katharine M. Rogers in *The Troublesome Helpmate*, p. 211.

13. Clarke's tract was entitled *Sex in Education.* See discussion by Elaine and English Showalter in "Victorian Women and Menstruation," in *Suffer and Be Still*, pp. 38–44.

14. Rogers, *The Troublesome Helpmate*, p. 213.

15. Adria Reich, "Teaching Is a Good Profession . . . For A Woman," in *And Jill Came Tumbling After*, p. 338.

16. Nancy Frazier and Myra Sadker, *Sexism in School and Society* (New York: Harper & Row, 1973), p. 96.

17. Pauline S. Sears and David H. Feldman, "Teacher Interactions with Boys and with Girls" and Betty Levy, "Do Schools Sell Girls Short?" in *And Jill Came Tumbling After*, pp. 147–158 and 142–146.

18. Elizabeth Janeway, *Man's World, Woman's Place*, p. 99.

19. Women on Words and Images, "Look Jane Look. See Sex Stereotypes," in *And Jill Came Tumbling After*, pp. 159–177.

20. See Elizabeth Fisher, "Children's Books: The Second Sex, Junior Division," and Marsha Federbush, "The Sex Problems of School Math Books," in *And Jill Came Tumbling After*, pp. 116–122 and 178–184. An overwhelming number of such studies have appeared, with particular attention being given to books adopted or recommended in state systems. See, for example, Marjorie B. U'Ren's "The Image of Women in Textbooks," in *Women in Sexist Society: Studies in Power and Powerlessness,* ed. Vivian Gornick and Barbara K. Moran (New York: New American Library, 1971), in which it is shown that, of texts adopted or recommended for second to sixth-grade use in California, 75 per cent of the main characters are male.

21. Alleen Pace Nilsen, "Women in Children's Literature," *College English*, 32 (May 1971), 920.

22. Epstein, *Woman's Place*, p. 23.

23. Michelle Patterson and Lucy Sells, "Women Dropouts from Higher Education," in *Academic Women on the Move*, p. 86.

CHAPTER 4. MEN, MANNERS, AND GAMESMANSHIP IN ACADEME

1. Betty E. Chmaj, *American Women and American Studies* (Pittsburgh: Know, 1971), p. 11.

2. Cf. Ch. 2 of Gertrude Himmelfarb's *Darwin and the Darwinian Revolution* (New York: Doubleday, 1962), esp. pp. 38–39, for one of the most amusing of the many accounts of Victorian educational eccentricities.

3. John Gross, *The Rise and Fall of the Man of Letters: A Study of the Idiosyncratic and the Humane in Modern Literature* (New York: Macmillan, 1969), p. 142.

4. Ben Morreale, *Down and Out in Academia* (New York: Pitman, 1972), p. 117.

5. Don Cameron Allen, *The Ph.D. in English and American Literature* (New York: Holt, Rinehart and Winston, 1968), p. 12.

6. Allen, p. 90.

7. From B. W. Kunkel, "A Survey of College Teachers," *Bulletin of the AAUP* 24 (1938), 262. Cited in Logan Wilson's *The Academic Man: A Study in the Sociology of a Profession* (London: Oxford University Press, 1942), p. 19.

8. Wilson, p. 19.

9. Helen S. Astin, *The Woman Doctorate in America: Origins, Career, and Family* (New York: Russell Sage Foundation, 1969), pp. 24–25.

10. Milton M. Gordon, "The Intellectual Subsociety," in Charles H. Anderson and John D. Murray, eds., *The Professors: Work and Life Styles Among Academicians* (Cambridge: Schenkman Publishing Co., 1971), p. 243.

11. Theodore Caplow and Reece J. McGee, *The Academic Marketplace* (New York: Basic Books, 1958), p. 226.

12. Oscar Butz, "Academic Freedom for What?" in Robert O. Bowen, ed., *The New Professors* (New York: Holt, Rinehart and Winston, 1960), p. 62; Vergilius Ferm, *Inside Ivy Walls: Observations from a College Professor's Notebook* (New York: Citadel Press, 1964), p. 135; Caplow and McGee, p. 228.

13. Morreale, p. 95.

14. Caplow and McGee, p. 45.

15. C. P. Snow, *The Two Cultures: And a Second Look* (New York: New American Library, 1963), p. 23.

16. Cf. Jessie Bernard's distinction between the teacher and the man of knowledge in *Academic Women* (University Park, Pa.: Penn. State University Press, 1964), pp. 115–120.

17. Jacques Barzun, *The American University: How It Runs, Where It Is Going* (New York: Harper & Row, 1968), p. 222.

18. Christopher Jencks and David Riesman, "The Art of Teaching," in Anderson and Murray, p. 63.

19. Lewis Coser, "Academic Intellectuals," in Anderson and Murray, p. 86.

20. Caplow and McGee, p. 72.

21. Paul F. Lazarsfeld and Wagner Thielens, Jr., *The Academic Mind: Social Scientists in a Time of Crisis* (Glencoe, Ill.: Free Press, 1958), p. 399.

22. Morreale, p. 56.

23. Lazarsfeld and Thielens, p. 65. Peter Schrag, in *The Decline of the Wasp* (New York: Simon & Schuster, 1971), p. 69, sees a correlation between the social ambition of "first-generation ethnic intellectuals" and their resentment of the freaks and members of the counter-culture who are threatening their too recently established position within the social elite.

24. Bertrand Russell, *The Autobiography of Bertrand Russell, 1914–1944* (New York: Bantam Books, 1969), p. 318.

25. Cf. Noel Perrin, *Dr. Bowdler's Legacy: A History of Expurgated Books in England and America* (New York: Doubleday, 1971), pp. 188–189.

CHAPTER 5. BELOW THE BELT AND INTO THE KIDNEYS: RITES OF
         PASSAGE

1. Astin, p. 107.

2. Caroline Bird, *Everything a Woman Needs to Know to Get Paid What She's Worth*, ed. Helene Mandelbaum (New York: David McKay, 1973), p. 10.

3. Chmaj, p. 3. Cf. also Nancy Jo Hoffman, "Sexism in Letters of Recommendation: A Case for Consciousness Raising," *MLA Newsletter*, 4 (September 1972), 6.

4. Cf. "Forum Newsfront," *Playboy*, 21 (March 1974), 50.

5. Caplow and McGee, p. 109.

6. Morreale, p. 94.

7. Wilson, pp. 54–55.

8. Michael Korda, *Male Chauvinism: How It Works* (New York: Random House, 1972), p. 33.

9. Hoffman, p. 5.

10. Hoffman, p. 5.

11. Simone de Beauvoir, *The Second Sex*, tr. H. M. Parshley (New York: Bantam Books, 1961), p. xxi.

12. Robert Bernard, *Deadly Meeting* (New York: Curtis, 1970), p. 41.

13. Astin, p. 72. Similar results have been produced by a number of other studies.

14. Caplow and McGee, p. 125.

15. Laura Morlock, "Discipline Variation in the Status of Women," in Rossi, *Academic Women on the Move*, p. 277.

16. Alice H. Cook, "Sex Discrimination at Universities: An Ombudsman's View," *AAUP Bulletin*, 58 (September 1972), 280.

CHAPTER 6. CHAOS IN THE CLASSROOM AND ELSEWHERE—
THE EARLY YEARS

1. Cynthia F. Epstein, "Encountering the Male Establishment: Sex-Status Limits on Women's Careers in the Professions," in *The Professional Woman*, ed. Athena Theodore (Cambridge: Schenkman, 1971), p. 66.
2. Patricia Albjerg Graham, "Women in Academe," in Theodore, pp. 722–723.
3. Alice S. Rossi, "Who Wants Women Scientists?" in *Women and the Scientific Professions: The M.I.T. Symposium on American Women in Science and Engineering*, ed. Jacquelyn A. Mattfeld and Carol G. Van Aken (Cambridge: M.I.T. Press, 1965), p. 65.
4. Epstein, "Encountering the Male Establishment," pp. 64–65.
5. Caroline Bird, *Everything a Woman Needs to Know*, p. 134.
6. Cf. *AAUP Bulletin*, 57 (March 1971), 50–52, 53–57; 54 (December 1968), 433–438; 57 (September 1971), 382–420; 55 (March 1969), 41–49.
7. Morlock, in *Academic Women on the Move*, p. 276.
8. Helen S. Astin and Alan E. Bayer, "Sex Discrimination in Academe," in *Academic Women on the Move*, p. 335.
9. Jessie Bernard, p. 154.
10. Morreale, p. 103.
11. Alan Wolfe, "Hard Times on Campus," in Anderson and Murray, p. 149.
12. Cf. Philip Goldberg, "Are Women Prejudiced Against Women?" in *And Jill Came Tumbling After*, pp. 40–41.
13. Korda, p. 34.
14. Agnes de Mille, p. 235.
15. Caroline Bird, *Born Female*, p. 49.
16. Korda, pp. 40–41.
17. Caplow and McGee, p. 78.
18. Eric Berne, *Games People Play: The Psychology of Human Relationships* (New York: Grove Press, 1964), p. 126.

CHAPTER 7. FROM FEMALE GRIEVANCE TO FEMINIST INSURRECTION

1. Georgina M. Smith, "Faculty Women at the Bargaining Table," *AAUP Bulletin*, 59 (December 1973), 403.
2. Betty Chmaj, p. 5.

3. J. Douglas Brown, *The Liberal University: An Institutional Analysis* (New York: McGraw-Hill, 1969), pp. 117–118.

4. Archie R. Dykes, *Faculty Participation in Academic Decision Making: Report of a Study* (Washington, D.C.: American Council on Education, 1968), pp. 2–3.

5. Jessie Bernard, *Academic Women,* p. 193.

6. Robert P. Quinn, Robert L. Kahn, Joyce M. Tabor and Laura K. Gordon, *The Chosen Few: A Study of Discrimination in Executive Selection* (Ann Arbor, Mich.: The University of Michigan Institute for Social Research Survey Research Center, 1968), p. 46.

7. Quinn, p. 28.

8. Quinn, p. 46.

9. Lora H. Robinson, "Institutional Variation in the Status of Academic Women," in *Academic Women on the Move,* p. 213.

10. D. B. Gowin and George H. Daigneault, *The Part-Time College Teacher* (Chicago: Center for the Study of Liberal Education for Adults, 1961), p. 4.

11. Georgina Smith, p. 404.

12. Kay Klotzburger, "Political Action by Academic Women," in *Academic Women on the Move,* pp. 369–372.

13. George Bernard Shaw, preface to *Man and Superman,* p. 32.

14. Caroline Bird, *Everything a Woman Needs to Know,* p. 248.

15. William Storrs Lee, *God Bless Our Queer Old Dean* (New York: Putnam, 1959), p. 177.

CHAPTER 8. TREADING THE WATERS OF OBLIVION

1. Caplow and McGee, p. 227.

2. Lora H. Robinson, in *Academic Women on the Move,* p. 215.

3. Caroline D. Eckhardt and John B. Smith, "Facts of Scholarly Publishing: Book-Length Works on Literature," *PMLA,* 89 (March 1974), 366.

4. Robinson, p. 224.

5. Jack Olsen, *The Girls on the Campus* (New York: Pocket Books, 1974), p. 211 ff.

6. George Bernard Shaw, from *Music in London,* as quoted by Stanley Weintraub (ed.) in *Shaw: An Autobiography, 1856–98* (New York: Weybright and Talley, 1969), p. 215.

7. Anna Jameson, *Characteristics of Women, Moral, Poetical and Historical* (Boston: Houghton Mifflin and Co., 1888), p. 236.

8. Berne, pp. 100–103.

CHAPTER 9. TOWARD A MORE PROMISING FUTURE

1. Thornstein Veblen, *The Theory of the Leisure Class*, intro. C. Wright Mills (New York: New American Library, 1953), p. 231.

2. J. Douglas Brown, p. xvii.

3. Louis Crompton, *Shaw the Dramatist* (Lincoln, Nebr.: University of Nebraska Press, 1969), pp. v–vi.

4. Jacquetta Hawkes, *The First Great Civilizations: Life in Mesopotamia, The Indus Valley, and Egypt* (New York: Knopf, 1973), p. xiv.